EXCELSIOR/REGENTS COLLEGE
EXAMINATIONS

THIS IS YOUR **PASSBOOK**® FOR ...

ESSENTIALS OF NURSING CARE: HEALTH DIFFERENCES

NATIONAL LEARNING CORPORATION®
passbooks.com

COPYRIGHT NOTICE

Copyright © 2018 by

NLC®

National Learning Corporation

212 Michael Drive, Syosset, NY 11791
(516) 921-8888 • www.passbooks.com
E-mail: info@passbooks.com

PUBLISHED IN THE UNITED STATES OF AMERICA

PASSBOOK® SERIES

THE *PASSBOOK® SERIES* has been created to prepare applicants and candidates for the ultimate academic battlefield – the examination room.

At some time in our lives, each and every one of us may be required to take an examination – for validation, matriculation, admission, qualification, registration, certification, or licensure.

Based on the assumption that every applicant or candidate has met the basic formal educational standards, has taken the required number of courses, and read the necessary texts, the *PASSBOOK® SERIES* furnishes the one special preparation which may assure passing with confidence, instead of failing with insecurity. Examination questions – together with answers – are furnished as the basic vehicle for study so that the mysteries of the examination and its compounding difficulties may be eliminated or diminished by a sure method.

This book is meant to help you pass your examination provided that you qualify and are serious in your objective.

The entire field is reviewed through the huge store of content information which is succinctly presented through a provocative and challenging approach – the question-and-answer method.

A climate of success is established by furnishing the correct answers at the end of each test.

You soon learn to recognize types of questions, forms of questions, and patterns of questioning. You may even begin to anticipate expected outcomes.

You perceive that many questions are repeated or adapted so that you can gain acute insights, which may enable you to score many sure points.

You learn how to confront new questions, or types of questions, and to attack them confidently and work out the correct answers.

You note objectives and emphases, and recognize pitfalls and dangers, so that you may make positive educational adjustments.

Moreover, you are kept fully informed in relation to new concepts, methods, practices, and directions in the field.

You discover that you arre actually taking the examination all the time: you are preparing for the examination by "taking" an examination, not by reading extraneous and/or supererogatory textbooks.

In short, this PASSBOOK®, used directedly, should be an important factor in helping you to pass your test.

EXCELSIOR/REGENTS COLLEGE EXAMINATIONS (E/RCE)

With Excelsior/Regents College Examinations, you can show what you know and earn the college-level credit you deserve. If you're like many adults today, you've worked hard to get where you are personally and professionally, and are working even harder to improve your situation. You're looking for a way to earn the college degree you've always wanted, and want your past training and experiences to apply toward that degree. Or perhaps you are interested in pursuing independent study in a subject for which Excelsior/Regents College Examinations offer credit. Either way, when you're ready, you can earn three or more credit hours with each Excelsior/Regents College Examination you take.

You don't have to be enrolled in Excelsior/Regents College to gain credit by examination. Credit earned by taking Excelsior/Regents College Examinations may be used at more than 900 other colleges and universities in the United States.

Excelsior/Regents College offers 32 highly respected degree programs for adult learners in Business, Liberal Arts, Nursing, and Technology. It's difficult for many adults to suspend life's everyday demands to go back to school. That's why the Excelsior/Regents College offers adult learners something unique—the opportunity to complete a degree without attending classes in a traditional college setting.

The Excelsior/Regents College degree programs combine independent study, classwork at colleges and universities throughout the world, coursework accomplished on the job, televised and Internet distance learning classes, and examinations for college credit like Excelsior/Regents College Examinations.

The Excelsior/Regents College specialize in providing adults a variety of ways to demonstrate the knowledge they've gained on the job or through past educational experiences and to earn college-level credit for it.

Excelsior/Regents College Examinations are college-level examinations that are used by more than 900 colleges and universities in the United States to award credit or advanced placement. Excelsior/Regents College Examinations provide flexible opportunities for adults to demonstrate their college-level knowledge in the arts and sciences, business, education, and nursing. They enable colleges to offer students options such as advanced placement and exemption from course requirements, and give employers a means to allow employees to earn credit toward job advancement or to pursue a college education without interrupting work schedules. Excelsior/Regents College Examinations credit has also been used toward teach certification or advancement and in fulfillment of civil service qualifications and continuing education requirements.

Registration

Registration materials for Excelsior/Regents College Examinations can be obtained by a variety of means. Detailed information about the administration of the exams, testing center locations, fees, provisions for international and reasonable accommodations testing, and complete instructions for registering are included in the free registration packet. Request the registration packet as follows:

Postal mail: The Administration
Regents College
7 Columbia Circle
Albany, New York 12203-5159

Telephone: 888-RCEXAMS

Fax: (518) 464-8777

E-mail: testadmin@regents.edu

TDD   (518) 464-8501

Web: www.regents.edu/804.htm

When you're ready to demonstrate what you've learned, you can complete the registration process by the traditional mail method or, for faster eligibility, register entirely by phone. Phone registration is very simple: Call 1-888-RCEXAMS, toll-free, to register using your credit card. Once your registration is complete, you will receive an Authorization to Test letter that will admit you to the Sylvan Technology Center you choose. You will have 90 days to schedule your exam by calling Sylvan directly, toll-free.

Test Development and Scoring

A committee of faculty determined the content to be tested on each Excelsior/Regents College examination. Committee members are teaching faculty and practicing professionals in the field covered by the exam. The Excelsior/Regents College Assessment Unit staff oversee the technical aspects of test construction in accordance with current professional standards.

Multiple-choice examinations may contain anywhere from 80 to 160 four-option multiple-choice questions, some of which are unscored, experimental questions. Extended response and mixed format examinations will have fewer questions that you must answer at some length. Since you will not be able to tell which questions are experimental, you should do your best on all of them. Scores are based on ability level as defined in the item response theory (IRT) method of examination development, rather than simply your total number of correct answers. Your score will be reported as a letter grade.

HOW TO TAKE A TEST

You have studied long, hard and conscientiously.

With your official admission card in hand, and your heart pounding, you have been admitted to the examination room.

You note that there are several hundred other applicants in the examination room waiting to take the same test.

They all appear to be equally well prepared.

You know that nothing but your best effort will suffice. The "moment of truth" is at hand: you now have to demonstrate objectively, in writing, your knowledge of content and your understanding of subject matter.

You are fighting the most important battle of your life—to pass and/or score high on an examination which will determine your career and provide the economic basis for your livelihood.

What extra, special things should you know and should you do in taking the examination?

I. YOU MUST PASS AN EXAMINATION

A. WHAT EVERY CANDIDATE SHOULD KNOW

Examination applicants often ask us for help in preparing for the written test. What can I study in advance? What kinds of questions will be asked? How will the test be given? How will the papers be graded?

B. HOW ARE EXAMS DEVELOPED?

Examinations are carefully written by trained technicians who are specialists in the field known as "psychological measurement," in consultation with recognized authorities in the field of work that the test will cover. These experts recommend the subject matter areas or skills to be tested; only those knowledges or skills important to your success on the job are included. The most reliable books and source materials available are used as references. Together, the experts and technicians judge the difficulty level of the questions.

Test technicians know how to phrase questions so that the problem is clearly stated. Their ethics do not permit "trick" or "catch" questions. Questions may have been tried out on sample groups, or subjected to statistical analysis, to determine their usefulness.

Written tests are often used in combination with performance tests, ratings of training and experience, and oral interviews. All of these measures combine to form the best-known means of finding the right person for the right job.

II. HOW TO PASS THE WRITTEN TEST

A. BASIC STEPS

1) Study the announcement

How, then, can you know what subjects to study? Our best answer is: "Learn as much as possible about the class of positions for which you've applied." The exam will test the knowledge, skills and abilities needed to do the work.

Your most valuable source of information about the position you want is the official exam announcement. This announcement lists the training and experience qualifications. Check these standards and apply only if you come reasonably close to meeting them. Many jurisdictions preview the written test in the exam announcement by including a section called "Knowledge and Abilities Required," "Scope of the Examination," or some similar heading. Here you will find out specifically what fields will be tested.

2) Choose appropriate study materials

If the position for which you are applying is technical or advanced, you will read more advanced, specialized material. If you are already familiar with the basic principles of your field, elementary textbooks would waste your time. Concentrate on advanced textbooks and technical periodicals. Think through the concepts and review difficult problems in your field.

These are all general sources. You can get more ideas on your own initiative, following these leads. For example, training manuals and publications of the government agency which employs workers in your field can be useful, particularly for technical and professional positions. A letter or visit to the government department involved may result in more specific study suggestions, and certainly will provide you with a more definite idea of the exact nature of the position you are seeking.

3) Study this book!

III. KINDS OF TESTS

Tests are used for purposes other than measuring knowledge and ability to perform specified duties. For some positions, it is equally important to test ability to make adjustments to new situations or to profit from training. In others, basic mental abilities not dependent on information are essential. Questions which test these things may not appear as pertinent to the duties of the position as those which test for knowledge and information. Yet they are often highly important parts of a fair examination. For very general questions, it is almost impossible to help you direct your study efforts. What we can do is to point out some of the more common of these general abilities needed in public service positions and describe some typical questions.

1) General information

Broad, general information has been found useful for predicting job success in some kinds of work. This is tested in a variety of ways, from vocabulary lists to questions about current events. Basic background in some field of work, such as sociology or economics, may be sampled in a group of questions. Often these are principles which have become familiar to most persons through exposure rather than through formal training. It is difficult to advise you how to study for these questions; being alert to the world around you is our best suggestion.

2) Verbal ability

An example of an ability needed in many positions is verbal or language ability. Verbal ability is, in brief, the ability to use and understand words. Vocabulary and grammar tests are typical measures of this ability. Reading comprehension or paragraph interpretation questions are common in many kinds of civil service tests. You are given a paragraph of written material and asked to find its central meaning.

IV. KINDS OF QUESTIONS

1. Multiple-choice Questions

Most popular of the short-answer questions is the "multiple choice" or "best answer" question. It can be used, for example, to test for factual knowledge, ability to solve problems or judgment in meeting situations found at work.

A multiple-choice question is normally one of three types:
- It can begin with an incomplete statement followed by several possible endings. You are to find the one ending which *best* completes the statement, although some of the others may not be entirely wrong.
- It can also be a complete statement in the form of a question which is answered by choosing one of the statements listed.
- It can be in the form of a problem – again you select the best answer.

Here is an example of a multiple-choice question with a discussion which should give you some clues as to the method for choosing the right answer:

When an employee has a complaint about his assignment, the action which will *best* help him overcome his difficulty is to
A. discuss his difficulty with his coworkers
B. take the problem to the head of the organization
C. take the problem to the person who gave him the assignment
D. say nothing to anyone about his complaint

In answering this question, you should study each of the choices to find which is best. Consider choice "A" – Certainly an employee may discuss his complaint with fellow employees, but no change or improvement can result, and the complaint remains unresolved. Choice "B" is a poor choice since the head of the organization probably does not know what assignment you have been given, and taking your problem to him is known as "going over the head" of the supervisor. The supervisor, or person who made the assignment, is the person who can clarify it or correct any injustice. Choice "C" is, therefore, correct. To say nothing, as in choice "D," is unwise. Supervisors have and interest in knowing the problems employees are facing, and the employee is seeking a solution to his problem.

2. True/False

3. Matching Questions
Matching an answer from a column of choices within another column.

V. RECORDING YOUR ANSWERS

Computer terminals are used more and more today for many different kinds of exams.

For an examination with very few applicants, you may be told to record your answers in the test booklet itself. Separate answer sheets are much more common. If this separate answer sheet is to be scored by machine – and this is often the case – it is highly important that you mark your answers correctly in order to get credit.

VI. BEFORE THE TEST

YOUR PHYSICAL CONDITION IS IMPORTANT
If you are not well, you can't do your best work on tests. If you are half asleep, you can't do your best either. Here are some tips:

1) Get about the same amount of sleep you usually get. Don't stay up all night before the test, either partying or worrying—DON'T DO IT!
2) If you wear glasses, be sure to wear them when you go to take the test. This goes for hearing aids, too.
3) If you have any physical problems that may keep you from doing your best, be sure to tell the person giving the test. If you are sick or in poor health, you relay cannot do your best on any test. You can always come back and take the test some other time.

Common sense will help you find procedures to follow to get ready for an examination. Too many of us, however, overlook these sensible measures. Indeed, nervousness and fatigue have been found to be the most serious reasons why applicants fail to do their best on civil service tests. Here is a list of reminders:

- Begin your preparation early – Don't wait until the last minute to go scurrying around for books and materials or to find out what the position is all about.
- Prepare continuously – An hour a night for a week is better than an all-night cram session. This has been definitely established. What is more, a night a week for a month will return better dividends than crowding your study into a shorter period of time.
- Locate the place of the exam – You have been sent a notice telling you when and where to report for the examination. If the location is in a different town or otherwise unfamiliar to you, it would be well to inquire the best route and learn something about the building.
- Relax the night before the test – Allow your mind to rest. Do not study at all that night. Plan some mild recreation or diversion; then go to bed early and get a good night's sleep.
- Get up early enough to make a leisurely trip to the place for the test – This way unforeseen events, traffic snarls, unfamiliar buildings, etc. will not upset you.

- Dress comfortably – A written test is not a fashion show. You will be known by number and not by name, so wear something comfortable.
- Leave excess paraphernalia at home – Shopping bags and odd bundles will get in your way. You need bring only the items mentioned in the official notice you received; usually everything you need is provided. Do not bring reference books to the exam. They will only confuse those last minutes and be taken away from you when in the test room.
- Arrive somewhat ahead of time – If because of transportation schedules you must get there very early, bring a newspaper or magazine to take your mind off yourself while waiting.
- Locate the examination room – When you have found the proper room, you will be directed to the seat or part of the room where you will sit. Sometimes you are given a sheet of instructions to read while you are waiting. Do not fill out any forms until you are told to do so; just read them and be prepared.
- Relax and prepare to listen to the instructions
- If you have any physical problem that may keep you from doing your best, be sure to tell the test administrator. If you are sick or in poor health, you really cannot do your best on the exam. You can come back and take the test some other time.

VII. AT THE TEST

The day of the test is here and you have the test booklet in your hand. The temptation to get going is very strong. Caution! There is more to success than knowing the right answers. You must know how to identify your papers and understand variations in the type of short-answer question used in this particular examination. Follow these suggestions for maximum results from your efforts:

1) Cooperate with the monitor

The test administrator has a duty to create a situation in which you can be as much at ease as possible. He will give instructions, tell you when to begin, check to see that you are marking your answer sheet correctly, and so on. He is not there to guard you, although he will see that your competitors do not take unfair advantage. He wants to help you do your best.

2) Listen to all instructions

Don't jump the gun! Wait until you understand all directions. In most civil service tests you get more time than you need to answer the questions. So don't be in a hurry. Read each word of instructions until you clearly understand the meaning. Study the examples, listen to all announcements and follow directions. Ask questions if you do not understand what to do.

3) Identify your papers

Civil service exams are usually identified by number only. You will be assigned a number; you must not put your name on your test papers. Be sure to copy your number correctly. Since more than one exam may be given, copy your exact examination title.

4) Plan your time

Unless you are told that a test is a "speed" or "rate of work" test, speed itself is usually not important. Time enough to answer all the questions will be provided, but this does not mean that you have all day. An overall time limit has been set. Divide the total time (in minutes) by the number of questions to determine the approximate time you have for each question.

5) Do not linger over difficult questions

If you come across a difficult question, mark it with a paper clip (useful to have along) and come back to it when you have been through the booklet. One caution if you do this – be sure to skip a number on your answer sheet as well. Check often to be sure that you have not lost your place and that you are marking in the row numbered the same as the question you are answering.

6) Read the questions

Be sure you know what the question asks! Many capable people are unsuccessful because they failed to *read* the questions correctly.

7) Answer all questions

Unless you have been instructed that a penalty will be deducted for incorrect answers, it is better to guess than to omit a question.

8) Speed tests

It is often better NOT to guess on speed tests. It has been found that on timed tests people are tempted to spend the last few seconds before time is called in marking answers at random – without even reading them – in the hope of picking up a few extra points. To discourage this practice, the instructions may warn you that your score will be "corrected" for guessing. That is, a penalty will be applied. The incorrect answers will be deducted from the correct ones, or some other penalty formula will be used.

9) Review your answers

If you finish before time is called, go back to the questions you guessed or omitted to give them further thought. Review other answers if you have time.

10) Return your test materials

If you are ready to leave before others have finished or time is called, take ALL your materials to the monitor and leave quietly. Never take any test material with you. The monitor can discover whose papers are not complete, and taking a test booklet may be grounds for disqualification.

VIII. EXAMINATION TECHNIQUES

1) Read the general instructions carefully. These are usually printed on the first page of the exam booklet. As a rule, these instructions refer to the timing of the examination; the fact that you should not start work until the signal and must stop work at a signal, etc. If there are any *special* instructions, such as a choice of questions to be answered, make sure that you note this instruction carefully.

2) When you are ready to start work on the examination, that is as soon as the signal has been given, read the instructions to each question booklet, underline any key words or phrases, such as *least, best, outline, describe*

and the like. In this way you will tend to answer as requested rather than discover on reviewing your paper that you *listed without describing*, that you selected the *worst* choice rather than the *best* choice, etc.

3) If the examination is of the objective or multiple-choice type – that is, each question will also give a series of possible answers: A, B, C or D, and you are called upon to select the best answer and write the letter next to that answer on your answer paper – it is advisable to start answering each question in turn. There may be anywhere from 50 to 100 such questions in the three or four hours allotted and you can see how much time would be taken if you read through all the questions before beginning to answer any. Furthermore, if you come across a question or group of questions which you know would be difficult to answer, it would undoubtedly affect your handling of all the other questions.

4) If the examination is of the essay type and contains but a few questions, it is a moot point as to whether you should read all the questions before starting to answer any one. Of course, if you are given a choice – say five out of seven and the like – then it is essential to read all the questions so you can eliminate the two that are most difficult. If, however, you are asked to answer all the questions, there may be danger in trying to answer the easiest one first because you may find that you will spend too much time on it. The best technique is to answer the first question, then proceed to the second, etc.

5) Time your answers. Before the exam begins, write down the time it started, then add the time allowed for the examination and write down the time it must be completed, then divide the time available somewhat as follows:
   - If 3-1/2 hours are allowed, that would be 210 minutes. If you have 80 objective-type questions, that would be an average of 2-1/2 minutes per question. Allow yourself no more than 2 minutes per question, or a total of 160 minutes, which will permit about 50 minutes to review.
   - If for the time allotment of 210 minutes there are 7 essay questions to answer, that would average about 30 minutes a question. Give yourself only 25 minutes per question so that you have about 35 minutes to review.

6) The most important instruction is to *read each question* and make sure you know what is wanted. The second most important instruction is to *time yourself properly* so that you answer every question. The third most important instruction is to *answer every question*. Guess if you have to but include something for each question. Remember that you will receive no credit for a blank and will probably receive some credit if you write something in answer to an essay question. If you guess a letter – say "B" for a multiple-choice question – you may have guessed right. If you leave a blank as an answer to a multiple-choice question, the examiners may respect your feelings but it will not add a point to your score. Some exams may penalize you for wrong answers, so in such cases *only*, you may not want to guess unless you have some basis for your answer.

7) Suggestions
   a. Objective-type questions
      1. Examine the question booklet for proper sequence of pages and questions
      2. Read all instructions carefully
      3. Skip any question which seems too difficult; return to it after all other questions have been answered
      4. Apportion your time properly; do not spend too much time on any single question or group of questions
      5. Note and underline key words – *all, most, fewest, least, best, worst, same, opposite,* etc.
      6. Pay particular attention to negatives
      7. Note unusual option, e.g., unduly long, short, complex, different or similar in content to the body of the question
      8. Observe the use of "hedging" words – *probably, may, most likely,* etc.
      9. Make sure that your answer is put next to the same number as the question
      10. Do not second-guess unless you have good reason to believe the second answer is definitely more correct
      11. Cross out original answer if you decide another answer is more accurate; do not erase until you are ready to hand your paper in
      12. Answer all questions; guess unless instructed otherwise
      13. Leave time for review

   b. Essay questions
      1. Read each question carefully
      2. Determine exactly what is wanted. Underline key words or phrases.
      3. Decide on outline or paragraph answer
      4. Include many different points and elements unless asked to develop any one or two points or elements
      5. Show impartiality by giving pros and cons unless directed to select one side only
      6. Make and write down any assumptions you find necessary to answer the questions
      7. Watch your English, grammar, punctuation and choice of words
      8. Time your answers; don't crowd material

8) Answering the essay question

Most essay questions can be answered by framing the specific response around several key words or ideas. Here are a few such key words or ideas:

M's: manpower, materials, methods, money, management
P's: purpose, program, policy, plan, procedure, practice, problems, pitfalls, personnel, public relations
a. Six basic steps in handling problems:
   1. Preliminary plan and background development
   2. Collect information, data and facts
   3. Analyze and interpret information, data and facts
   4. Analyze and develop solutions as well as make recommendations

5. Prepare report and sell recommendations
6. Install recommendations and follow up effectiveness

b. Pitfalls to avoid
1. *Taking things for granted* – A statement of the situation does not necessarily imply that each of the elements is necessarily true; for example, a complaint may be invalid and biased so that all that can be taken for granted is that a complaint has been registered
2. *Considering only one side of a situation* – Wherever possible, indicate several alternatives and then point out the reasons you selected the best one
3. *Failing to indicate follow up* – Whenever your answer indicates action on your part, make certain that you will take proper follow-up action to see how successful your recommendations, procedures or actions turn out to be
4. *Taking too long in answering any single question* – Remember to time your answers properly

EXAMINATION SECTION

EXAMINATION SECTION

TEST 1

DIRECTIONS: Each question or incomplete statement is followed by several suggested answers or completions. Select the one that BEST answers the question or completes the statement. *PRINT THE LETTER OF THE CORRECT ANSWER IN THE SPACE AT THE RIGHT.*

1. What assistive device will prevent external rotation of the hip when the patient is lying in the supine position?
   A. Abductor pillow
   B. Ankle roll
   C. Trochanter roll
   D. Knee splint

   1._____

2. What clinical manifestation is indicative of a fecal impaction?
   A. Seepage of liquid stool
   B. Flatulence
   C. Tarry stools
   D. Bloody stools

   2._____

3. What serum electrolyte value will be elevated in a patient who has been immobilized for an extended period?
   A. Calcium
   B. Magnesium
   C. Sodium
   D. Potassium

   3._____

4. Which medical condition can be caused by gastric suctioning?
   A. Metabolic alkalosis
   B. Metabolic acidosis
   C. Respiratory acidosis
   D. Respiratory alkalosis

   4._____

5. Use of aminoglycoside antibiotics is a risk factor for what medical condition?
   A. Hyperkalemia
   B. Hypomagnesemia
   C. Hypercalcemia
   D. Hypoglycemia

   5._____

6. Which medical condition can occur if an athlete loses large amounts of water and salt in sweat and replaces the loss with water alone?
   A. Hyperchloremia
   B. Hypoglycemia
   C. Hyponatremia
   D. Hyperkalemia

   6._____

7. What electrolyte imbalance is associated with Trousseau's and Chvostek's signs, skeletal muscle irritability, muscle cramping, and possible tetany?
   A. Hyponatremia
   B. Hypomagnesemia
   C. Hypocalcemia
   D. Hypokalemia

   7._____

8. What isotonic alkalinizing solution should be to rehydrate the cells of a patient with metabolic acidosis?
   A. Lactated Ringers solution
   B. Lugols solution
   C. Normal saline solution
   D. D5W solution

   8._____

9. Which of the following is a volume expander used to treat severe loss of blood or plasma?
   A. Lactated Ringers solution
   B. Lugols solution
   C. Normal saline solution
   D. Human serum albumin

9.____

10. _____ is a loop diuretic indicated for treatment of edema.
   A. Kayexalate   B. Furosemide   C. Triamterene   D. Spironolactone

10.____

11. _____ incontinence occurs when the urinary tract is intact and able to function but the patient is cognitively unable to identify the need to void.
   A. Urge   B. Functional   C. Reflex   D. Stress

11.____

12. Involuntary urination due to a bladder that is not emptying normally and becomes very distended is referred to as _____ incontinence.
   A. functional   B. reflex   C. stress   D. overflow

12.____

13. Insufficient insulin, severe exercise, exposure to cold, and loss of carbohydrates can result in _____ being present in the urine.
   A. proteins   B. glucose   C. ketones   D. red blood cells

13.____

14. What color of stool is considered normal for an infant who is breastfed?
   A. Yellow   B. Green   C. Orange   D. Black

14.____

15. Which of the following is an abnormal breathing pattern characterized by deep, gasping inspiration followed by a brief, insufficient release which is caused by damage to the pons or upper medulla caused by strokes or trauma?
   A. Cheyne Stokes respirations
   B. Apneustic respirations
   C. Biot's respirations
   D. Kussmaul's respirations

15.____

16. _____ is an abnormal pattern of breathing characterized by groups of quick, shallow inspirations followed by regular or irregular periods of apnea caused by damage to the medulla oblongata due to strokes, trauma, or CNS dysfunction.
   A. Cheyne Stokes respirations
   B. Apneustic respirations
   C. Biot's respirations
   D. Kussmaul's respirations

16.____

17. What type of breathing is associated with metabolic acidosis, ketoacidosis, renal failure, shock, and lactic acidosis as the body seeks to rid itself of excess CO_2?
   A. Cheyne Stokes respirations
   B. Apneustic respirations
   C. Biot's respirations
   D. Kussmaul's respirations

17.____

18. When assessing skin turgor on a 15-year-old male, where should the nurse pinch the skin?
   A. Upper arm   B. Inner thigh   C. Face   D. Abdomen

18.____

19.

Which medical condition is illustrated by the above electrocardiogram?
A. Hypercalcemia
B. Hyponatremia
C. Hyperkalemia
D. Hypomagnesemia

19.____

20. Bruising all over the body and bleeding gums is an indication of deficiency of vitamin
A. A
B. B6
C. B12
D. C

20.____

21. Which of the following results in reduction in joint flexibility?
A. Loss of cartilage
B. Bone demineralization
C. Vitamin D deficiency
D. Calcium deficiency

21.____

22. Which serum electrolyte will be elevated in a patient with diabetes insipidus?
A. Calcium
B. Sodium
C. Magnesium
D. Potassium

22.____

23. Which of the following medications can cause green/gray colored stools due to impaired digestion?
A. Augmentin
B. Iron salts
C. Antacids
D. Antibiotics

23.____

24. Which of the following is responsible for regulating calcium and phosphorus in the human body?
A. Thyroid stimulating hormone
B. Parathyroid hormone
C. Aldosterone
D. Adiponectin

24.____

25. Bronchitis is caused by a
A. fungus
B. bacteria
C. virus
D. prion

25.____

KEY (CORRECT ANSWERS)

1.	C		11.	A
2.	A		12.	D
3.	A		13.	C
4.	A		14.	A
5.	B		15.	B
6.	C		16.	C
7.	C		17.	D
8.	A		18.	D
9.	D		19.	C
10.	B		20.	D

21.	A
22.	B
23.	D
24.	B
25.	C

TEST 2

DIRECTIONS: Each question or incomplete statement is followed by several suggested answers or completions. Select the one that BEST answers the question or completes the statement. *PRINT THE LETTER OF THE CORRECT ANSWER IN THE SPACE AT THE RIGHT.*

1. What medical condition is characterized by chronic damage to the alveoli, causing them to over inflate?
   A. Asthma   B. Emphysema   C. Bronchitis   D. Orthopnea

   1.____

2. What is the MOST common causative organism of urinary tract infections?
   A. Escherichia coli   B. Listeria monocytogenes
   C. Salmonella typhi   D. Staphylococcus aureus

   2.____

3. _____ diet is a nutritional consideration which should be addressed for a patient with Addison's disease?
   A. High sodium   B. Low sodium
   C. High potassium   D. Low potassium

   3.____

4. Which of the following is the preferred source of energy for the heart?
   A. Glucose   B. Fats
   C. Carbohydrates   D. Fatty acids

   4.____

5. Deficiency of which mineral leads to microcytic anemia, decreased work capacity, fatigue, weakness, and spoon-shaped cells?
   A. Potassium   B. Iron   C. Selenium   D. Manganese

   5.____

6. Deficiency of _____ leads to muscle pain, heart enlargement, and heart failure.
   A. potassium   B. iron   C. selenium   D. manganese

   6.____

7. Deficiencies of which vitamin leads to oral lesions, dermatitis, cracks in the corner of the mouth, red and swollen tongue, and reddening of the cornea?
   A. Pyridoxine   B. Thiamine   C. Riboflavin   D. Cobalamin

   7.____

8. Which salivary enzyme starts the digestion of starches in the mouth?
   A. Pepsin   B. Ptyalin   C. Dextrin   D. Lipase

   8.____

9. Which mineral facilitates glucose uptake b cells and decreases serum cholesterol and triglycerides?
   A. Chromium   B. Iodine   C. Chloride   D. Zinc

   9.____

10. Which mineral functions in tissue growth, development and healing, sexual maturation and reproduction, enzyme formation, and immune response?
    A. Iron   B. Zinc   C. Sulfur   D. Copper

    10.____

11. The mineral _____ is a component of cartilage, tendons, hair, and nails.   11._____
    A. zinc   B. copper   C. sulfur   D. selenium

12. Which of the following represents normal pCO$_2$ values?   12._____
    A. 25-35 mmHg   B. 35-45 mmHg   C. 45-55 mmHg   D. 55-65 mmHg

13. Which of the following represents normal pO$_2$ values?   13._____
    A. 40-60 mmHg   B. 60-80 mmHg
    C. 80-100 mmHg   D. 100-120 mmHg

14. Which of the following is characterized by passive movement of fluid across   14._____
    a membrane from lower solute concentration to higher solute concentration?
    A. Diffusion   B. Osmosis
    C. Active transport   D. Absorption

15. Which of the following is a cause of respiratory alkalosis?   15._____
    A. Starvation   B. Vomiting
    C. Prolonged NG tube suctioning   D. Anxiety

16. What vaccine is contraindicated for a child who is HIV seropositive and   16._____
    severely immunocompromised?
    A. Influenza   B. Chickenpox   C. Rubella   D. DTAP

17. Which clinical manifestation is MOST indicative of Lyme disease in children?   17._____
    A. Petechiae
    B. Ring-shaped rash
    C. Koplik's spots on buccal mucosa
    D. Abdominal distention

18. Which area of the brain is responsible for vision?   18._____
    A. Parietal   B. Occipital   C. Frontal   D. Cerebellum

19. A patient who has sustained a complete spinal cord transection at level C4   19._____
    will MOST likely have which medical condition?
    A. Paraplegia   B. Quadriplegia
    C. Respiratory failure   D. Urinary incontinence

20. Which area of the brain is the major receiving area for sensory nerves?   20._____
    A. Thalamus   B. Hypothalamus
    C. Cerebrum   D. Cerebellum

21. What assistive device is used to prevent the internal rotation of the femur?   21._____
    A. Trochanter roll   B. Abductor pillow
    C. Ankle roll   D. Knee splint

22. Which of the following measures the body's ability to carry oxygen?   22._____
    A. Hemoglobin level   B. Hematocrit level
    C. Red blood cell count   D. White blood cell count

23. _____ is characterized by retraction of the skin of the prepuce causing painful swelling of the skin of the glans penis that prevents the penis from being retracted.
    A. Priapism   B. Paraphimosis
    C. Peyronie's disease   D. Balanitis
23.____

24. If a patient is receiving a thiazide diuretic for treatment of fluid volume excess related to hypernatremia, what observation would indicate the medication is having the desired effect?
    A. Increased blood pressure   B. Decreased blood pressure
    C. Weight loss   D. Weight gain
24.____

25. Treatment of which of the following pharmacological agents may result in magnesium and water imbalance?
    A. Antacids   B. Glucocorticoids
    C. NSAIDS   D. Antibiotics
25.____

KEY (CORRECT ANSWERS)

1.	B	11.	C
2.	A	12.	B
3.	A	13.	C
4.	D	14.	B
5.	B	15.	D
6.	C	16.	C
7.	C	17.	B
8.	B	18.	B
9.	A	19.	B
10.	B	20.	A

21.	B
22.	A
23.	B
24.	B
25.	D

TEST 3

DIRECTIONS: Each question or incomplete statement is followed by several suggested answers or completions. Select the one that BEST answers the question or completes the statement. *PRINT THE LETTER OF THE CORRECT ANSWER IN THE SPACE AT THE RIGHT.*

1.   A decrease in 250 calories per day will cause how much weight loss per week?   1.____
    A. 0.5 lbs.   B. 1.0 lbs.   C. 1.5 lbs.   D. 2.0 lbs.

2.   Which finding is characteristic of left sided heart failure?   2.____
    A. Bradycardia   B. Tachycardia
    C. Hypertension   D. Dyspnea on exertion

3.   Which of the following is recommended for precise regulation of oxygen delivery?   3.____
    A. Nasal cannula   B. Venturi mask
    C. Non-rebreather mask   D. Partial rebreather mask

4.   What is the appropriate device used to deliver oxygen at a rate of 2-3 L/min.?   4.____
    A. Nasal cannula   B. Venturi mask
    C. Non-rebreather mask   D. Partial rebreather mask

5.   Treatment with which pharmacologic agent may result in a sodium and water imbalance?   5.____
    A. Antacids   B. Glucocorticoids
    C. NSAIDS   D. Antibiotics

6.   Prior to suctioning the nasopharyngeal cavity of a patient who is unconscious, the nurse should place the patient in the _____ position.   6.____
    A. supine   B. upright   C. lateral   D. recumbent

7.   Which organ of the gastrointestinal system absorbs water and nutrients?   7.____
    A. Stomach   B. Liver
    C. Small intestine   D. Large intestine

8.   _____ is defined as persistent passing of stools into clothing in a child older than age 4 and incontinence would be expected.   8.____
    A. Encopresis   B. Parcopresis   C. Catachresis   D. Eisegesis

9.   What clinical manifestation is an early indicator of hypoxia?   9.____
    A. Bradypnea   B. Tachypnea   C. Orthopnea   D. Hypercapnia

10.   _____ is defined as greater than normal amounts of carbon dioxide in the blood ($PaCO_2 > 45$).   10.____
    A. Bradypnea   B. Tachypnea   C. Orthopnea   D. Hypercapnia

11. _____ are substances that have three fatty acids and account for over 90% of the lipids in food and in the body.

    A. Triglycerides   B. Lipoproteins

    C. Monosaccharides   D. Polysaccharides

11.____

12. Which vitamin is ESSENTIAL for producing certain blood clotting proteins?

    A. C   B. D   C. E   D. K

12.____

13. People with panic disorders have a high probability of developing which medical condition?

    A. Tachycardia   B. Shortness of breath

    C. Palpitations   D. Mitral valve prolapse

13.____

14. Excessive alcohol consumption will deplete the bodily storage of which vitamin?

    A. A   B. B   C. D   D. K

14.____

15. Low levels of _____ indicates increased fluid, anemia, and protein-calorie malnutrition.

    A. Hemoglobin   B. Hematocrit

    C. Creatinine   D. Blood urea nitrogen

15.____

16. One unit of red blood cells increases hematocrit by what percentage?

    A. 2%   B. 4%   C. 6%   D. 8%

16.____

17. Which of the following represents a normal value for urine specific gravity?

    A. 0.990-1.005   B. 1.005-1.030   C. 1.030-1.055   D. 1.055-1.080

17.____

18. Which of the following is the MOST common problem seen in the standing position of an adult which is characterized by an inward curvature of a portion of the lumbar and cervical vertebral column?

    A. Kyphosis   B. Scoliosis   C. Lordosis   D. Orthosis

18.____

19. _____ are white, shiny, flexible bands of fibrous tissue that connect bones to bones and provides strength and flexibility of the skeleton.

    A. Ligaments   B. Tendons   C. Cartilage   D. Muscle fibers

19.____

20. Which of the following is a non-vascular, supporting, connective tissue that is located chiefly in the joints and in the nose, ear, thorax, trachea, and larynx that provides strength and flexibility of the skeleton?

    A. Ligaments   B. Tendons   C. Cartilage   D. Muscle fibers

20.____

21. When assessing skin turgor, a delay in the skin to return to normal is referred to as

    A. pinching   B. tenting   C. nesting   D. clumping

21.____

22. Which heart sound represents the end of systole?

    A. S1   B. S2   C. S3   D. S4

22.____

23. _____ is defined as coordinated, rhythmic, serial contractions of the smooth muscles of the GI tract.

    A. Mastication   B. Deglutition   C. Peristalsis   D. Absorption

23.____

24. Which of the following classes of nutrients are required to supply energy?

    A. Vitamins   B. Minerals   C. Water   D. Proteins

24.____

25. Which of the following classes of nutrients are required to regulate body processes?

    A. Lipids   B. Vitamins
    C. Carbohydrates   D. Proteins

25.____

KEY (CORRECT ANSWERS)

1.	A		11.	A
2.	D		12.	D
3.	B		13.	D
4.	A		14.	B
5.	B		15.	B
6.	C		16.	B
7.	D		17.	B
8.	A		18.	C
9.	B		19.	A
10.	D		20.	C

21.	B
22.	B
23.	C
24.	D
25.	B

TEST 4

DIRECTIONS: Each question or incomplete statement is followed by several suggested answers or completions. Select the one that BEST answers the question or completes the statement. *PRINT THE LETTER OF THE CORRECT ANSWER IN THE SPACE AT THE RIGHT.*

1. Which disease should the nurse suspect when the child exhibits a white tongue with red papillae and a diffuse red rash under the folds of the joints?
   A. Lyme disease   B. Measles   C. Scarlet fever   D. Chickenpox

   1.____

2. Which observation is indicative of the onset of sepsis in a patient with a gram negative infection?
   A. Hyperthermia   B. Hypothermia   C. Jaundice   D. Diaphoresis

   2.____

3. What is the MOST reliable method for accurately diagnosing a patient with active pulmonary tuberculosis?
   A. Chest x-ray   B. Urinalysis
   C. Blood culture   D. Sputum culture

   3.____

4. If a child has a family history of convulsions, what medication should be administered along with the diphtheria, tetanus, and pertussis immunization?
   A. Amoxicillin   B. Penicillin
   C. Acetaminophen   D. Naproxen

   4.____

5. Opportunistic infection, such as oral candidiasis, is a common problem associated with which infectious disease?
   A. Hepatitis C   B. HIV/AIDS   C. Tuberculosis   D. Smallpox

   5.____

6. Upon examination of a 13-year-old patient, you notice that one side of the rib cage is higher when the patient bends forward. What is your diagnosis based on this finding?
   A. Kyphosis   B. Scoliosis   C. Lordosis   D. Orthosis

   6.____

7. What type of exercise helps to maintain muscle tone in the forearm of a patient who is in a shoulder-to-waist cast?
   A. Isotonic   B. Isokinetic   C. Isometric   D. Anaerobic

   7.____

8. Which finding indicates that drug therapy for a patient with chronic gout has been effective?
   A. Normal BUN/Creatinine
   B. Normal erythrocyte sedimentation rate
   C. Normal WBC count
   D. Normal serum uric acid

   8.____

9. The symptoms of myasthenia gravis are thought to be caused by an impairment of the transmission of acetylcholine and usually related to a disorder in the _____ gland.
   A. Thyroid   B. Thymus   C. Parotid   D. Thalamus

   9.____

10. Following a craniotomy utilizing a transsphenoidal approach, the nurse should maintain the patient in what position?
    A. Prone   B. Supine   C. Upright   D. Recumbent

10.____

11. In which area should a nurse measure a patient's core body temperature during a surgical procedure?
    A. Orally   B. Rectally
    C. Forehead   D. Tympanic membrane

11.____

12. Which laboratory test result indicates that the condition of a patient with ulcerative colitis is improving?
    A. Decreasing hematocrit
    B. Decreasing hemoglobin
    C. Decreasing red blood cell count
    D. Decreasing erythrocyte sedimentation rate

12.____

13. Which body system experiences the MOST serious and irreversible side effects of lead poisoning?
    A. Nervous   B. Integumentary
    C. Gastrointestinal   D. Musculoskeletal

13.____

14. What is a clinical manifestation of smoke inhalation?
    A. Shortness of breath   B. Hyperventilation
    C. Acute hoarseness   D. Tachypnea

14.____

15. Which pathophysiological factor accounts for the increased incidence of opportunistic infections and tumors among patients with acquired immuno-deficiency syndrome?
Decreased number of
    A. macrophages   B. basophils   C. eosinophils   D. helper T cells

15.____

16. Which class of medication is generally administered to reduce cerebral edema?
    A. Diuretics   B. Antibiotics
    C. Corticosteroids   D. Glucocorticoids

16.____

17. When initiating total parenteral nutrition, it is critical for the nurse to monitor for which complication?
    A. Hyperglycemia   B. Hypoglycemia
    C. IV infiltration   D. Metabolic acidosis

17.____

18. What finding in the patient's lower extremity should lead the nurse to suspect venous insufficiency?
    A. Discoloration   B. Swelling/edema
    C. Hyperthermia   D. Leathery texture

18.____

19. Which method of oxygen delivery provides the patient with an oxygen concentration of greater than 80 percent?
    A. Nasal cannula   B. Venturi mask
    C. Non-rebreather mask   D. Partial rebreather mask

19.____

20. A patient with polycythemia is most at risk for developing which medical condition?
    A. Hypertension   B. Peptic ulcers
    C. Blood clots   D. Atherosclerosis

20.____

21. Which vitamin is MOST often lost during food preparation?
    A. A   B. C   C. D   D. K

21.____

22. What beverage should be taken with a ferrous sulfate capsule to triple the absorption rate of iron?
    A. Water   B. Tea   C. Milk   D. Orange juice

22.____

23. What nutrient does total parenteral nutrition provide that routine intravenous therapy solutions do not?
    A. Water   B. Electrolytes   C. Dextrose   D. Vitamins

23.____

24. The digestion and absorption of nutrients occurs PRIMARILY in which organ?
    A. Stomach   B. Liver
    C. Small intestine   D. Large intestine

24.____

25. Which of the following is defined as involuntary urination in children beyond the age when voluntary control is normal?
    A. Dysuria   B. Oliguria   C. Nocturia   D. Enuresis

25.____

KEY (CORRECT ANSWERS)

1.	C		11.	D
2.	A		12.	D
3.	D		13.	A
4.	C		14.	C
5.	B		15.	D
6.	B		16.	C
7.	C		17.	A
8.	D		18.	D
9.	D		19.	C
10.	B		20.	C

21.	B
22.	D
23.	C
24.	C
25.	D

EXAMINATION SECTION
TEST 1

DIRECTIONS: Each question or incomplete statement is followed by several suggested
answers or completions. Select the one that BEST answers the question or
completes the statement. *PRINT THE LETTER OF THE CORRECT ANSWER
IN THE SPACE AT THE RIGHT.*

Questions 1-6.

DIRECTIONS: Questions 1 through 6 are to be answered on the basis of the following information.

A 35-year-old black male is admitted to the ICU with intense, crushing, substernal chest
pain. According to the patient, the pain started about 40 minutes earlier and is not relieved by
nitroglycerin. The patient has had two bouts of vomiting, which contain the previous night's
food particles. The patient is a smoker and is mildly obese.

1. Nursing interventions to decrease the patient's cardiac workload include all of the follow-   1._____
    ing EXCEPT to

    A. administer oxygen as needed
    B. ask the patient to perform valsalva's maneuver
    C. give diuretics as ordered to reduce circulating blood volume
    D. prevent constipation and reduce anxiety

2. Nursing interventions to keep the patient free from new blood vessel occlusion would   2._____
    NOT include

    A. applying anti-embolic hose
    B. vigorous massage of extremities
    C. giving anticoagulants
    D. advising the patient on ankle flexion exercises

3. The nurse should interpret all of the following ECG findings as significant EXCEPT   3._____

    A. a P-R interval from 12 to 20 seconds
    B. elevation of the S-T segment
    C. inversion of T waves
    D. the appearance of pathological Q waves

4. In developing a discharge plan for a patient with a myocardial infarction, nursing goals   4._____
    should include

    A. restoring the patient to his optimal physiological, psychological, social, and work
        levels
    B. eliminating all risk factors
    C. entering the patient in an intensive program of occupational therapy
    D. all of the above

5. Nursing interventions to provide care after a percutaneous transluminal coronary angio-   5.____
plasty do NOT include

    A. monitoring pulses distal to puncture site
    B. monitoring arterial puncture site for bleeding
    C. keeping foot of bed elevated
    D. all of the above

6. Laboratory studies helpful in the diagnosis of this patient include all of the following   6.____
EXCEPT

    A. maximal level of CPK achieved 12-24 hours after the onset of symptoms
    B. decreased white blood cells
    C. LDH remains elevated for 5-7 days
    D. elevated sedimentation rate

Questions 7-10.

DIRECTIONS: Questions 7 through 10 are to be answered on the basis of the following information.

A 45-year-old black male comes to the hospital with complaints of generalized headache
and palpitations. According to the patient, headaches started about 3 days before, are severe
in intensity and are not accompanied by any chest pain, of shortness of breath, vomiting or
impairment of consciousness. Palpitations started the previous day. On examination, his
pulse is 89, blood pressure is 185/110, and respiratory rate is 23/minute.

7. Nursing roles in the education of this patient include advising him on all of the following   7.____
EXCEPT

    A. remaining on a salt-restricted diet
    B. lying flat in bed to avoid orthostatic hypertension
    C. reducing calories and losing weight
    D. practicing moderation in the use of coffee and alcohol

8. In the differential diagnosis of this condition, all of the following should be included   8.____
EXCEPT

    A. essential hypertension   B. renal disease
    C. coarctation of the aorta   D. hypothyroidism

9. In the diagnostic work-up of this patient, all of the following should be done EXCEPT   9.____

    A. serum cholesterol and triglycerides
    B. fasting blood glucose
    C. serum ammonium concentration
    D. urinalysis

10. Nursing implementations for a patient carrying out self-care activities after discharge   10.____
include

    A. taking own blood pressure   B. eliminating fats from the diet
    C. reducing weight by 20%   D. all of the above

Questions 11-14.

DIRECTIONS: Questions 11 through 14 are to be answered on the basis of the following information.

A 32-year-old white patient is admitted to the floor with a diagnosis of unstable angina. In trying to reach a definitive diagnosis, cardiac catheterization is planned.

11. Pre-catheterization nursing interventions for this patient do NOT include   11._____

   A. explaining the procedure to the patient and his family
   B. administering epidural anesthetics
   C. teaching relaxation techniques
   D. all of the above

12. After catheterization, the patient is diaphoretic and exhibits tachypnea, wheezing, tachy-   12._____
    cardia, and pallor. Nursing interventions in this case include all of the following EXCEPT

   A. encouraging increased fluid intake
   B. checking patient's output frequently
   C. adding 35 meq. KCl in every D5 drip
   D. observing for signs of hypovolemia

13. Nursing guides for self-management by the patient, after cardiac catheterization, include   13._____
    all of the following EXCEPT

   A. watching for bleeding or swelling at dressing sites
   B. decreasing fluid intake for 24 hours
   C. observing for signs of circulatory impairment of the extremities, such as discolora-
      tion, numbness, tingling, or lack of warmth
   D. expecting some pain at the site and taking pain medication

14. In order to prevent stress on an incision line, nursing advice should include   14._____

   A. no bending of affected limb
   B. no ambulation for 12-24 hours if femoral site is involved
   C. feeling temperature in area distal to operation site
   D. all of the above

Questions 15-22.

DIRECTIONS: Questions 15 through 22 are to be answered on the basis of the following information.

A 43-year-old male comes to the hospital with dyspnea and orthopnea. According to the patient, symptoms started about 10 days before and gradually the dyspnea became severe. On examination, ankle edema is present and neck veins are distended. On auscultation, pulmonary rales and third heart sounds are present.

15. This history is MOST consistent with a diagnosis of   15._____

   A. congestive heart failure   B. coarctation of the aorta
   C. hyperthyroidism   D. all of the above

16. Nursing interventions for the elimination of excess fluid in this patient include   16.____

    A. giving diuretics as ordered
    B. limiting fluid intake to 500 ml per day
    C. eliminating sodium intake
    D. all of the above

17. Symptoms indicative of right side congestive cardiac failure include all of the following   17.____
EXCEPT

    A. peripheral pitting edema
    B. dyspnea
    C. hepatomegaly
    D. distended neck veins

18. Nursing interventions to establish a balance between oxygen supply and demand include   18.____

    A. scheduling 30 minute sessions of cardiovascular exercise daily
    B. giving appropriate sedation to relieve nighttime anxiety and to provide restful sleep
    C. supplying oxygen through a nasal cannula
    D. all of the above

19. Upon discharge, the nurse should advise the patient to be alert to all of the following   19.____
signs and symptoms of recurrence EXCEPT

    A. swelling of ankles, feet, or abdomen
    B. loss in weight
    C. persistent cough
    D. frequent urination at night

20. All of the following complications may be expected in a patient with congestive cardiac   20.____
failure EXCEPT

    A. cardiac dysrhythmias   B. digitalis toxicity
    C. restrictive myocarditis   D. pulmonary infarction

21. If the same patient develops pulmonary edema, nursing interventions to keep the patient   21.____
adequately oxygenated do NOT include

    A. placing the patient in the prone position
    B. administering oxygen as ordered
    C. preparing to assist with phlebotomy if indicated
    D. all of the above

22. Nursing interventions to keep the patient free from the hazards of immobility include all of   22.____
the following EXCEPT

    A. advising the patient to avoid deep breathing and coughing
    B. turning frequently
    C. providing passive range of motion exercises as needed
    D. providing good back care

23. A patient with cardiopulmonary arrest is brought to the emergency room by EMS. The patient is breathless and unresponsive.
Nursing interventions to keep the airway open so that patient receives adequate ventilation include

    A. placing the patient in an upright sitting position
    B. performing an emergency tracheotomy
    C. opening the airway by head tilt-chin lift maneuver
    D. all of the above

23.____

24. Shock is a state in which tissue perfusion is not sufficient to sustain life.
Precipitating factors for shock include all of the following EXCEPT

    A. myocardial infarction   B. spinal anesthesia
    C. pneumonia   D. burns

24.____

25. The body's responses to shock include all of the following EXCEPT stimulation of

    A. the adrenal medualla by sympathetic nervous system
    B. the pancreas and secretion of insulin
    C. the renin-angiotensin-aldosterone system and anti-diuretic hormone
    D. cortisol and growth hormone secretions

25.____

26. Nursing interventions in a patient with shock, to ensure adequate perfusion, include

    A. monitoring blood pressure, pulse, respiration, and CVP
    B. maintaining urine output of at least 30 ml/hour and equal to intake
    C. administering blood, colloid fluids or electrolyte solution as necessary
    D. all of the above

26.____

27. In a patient with shock, nursing interventions to keep him protected from injury and complications do NOT include

    A. turning frequently to prevent decubitus ulcers and pulmonary problems
    B. wrist and ankle restraints
    C. using sterile techniques with all procedures, since patient has decreased resistance to infection
    D. keeping bed's side rails up; if patient is confused, watch carefully and avoid restraints

27.____

Questions 28-33.

DIRECTIONS: Questions 28 through 33 are to be answered on the basis of the following information.

A 28-year-old smoker is admitted with chronic cough and expectoration, episodic dyspnea, and weight gain. Physical examination shows hyperinflation, poor diaphragmatic movement, use of accessory muscles of respiration, decreased breath sounds and wheezing on auscultation. X-ray shows loss of vascularity, a flattened diaphragm, and a small heart.

28. Nursing evaluation of the predisposing factors for the above condition include

    A. smoking   B. poor diet
    C. an adolescent case of pneumonia   D. all of the above

28.____

29. Nursing interventions to maintain a PO$_2$ of at least 60 mmHg, a clear airway, and thin and   29.____
    clear sputum include all of the following EXCEPT

    A. administering bronchodilators and expectorants as ordered
    B. teaching relaxation techniques and breathing exercises
    C. administering high concentrations of humidified oxygen
    D. encouraging activity to tolerance

30. The nurse should advise the patient to avoid bed rest, if at all possible, to prevent all of   30.____
    the following EXCEPT

    A. stasis of secretions
    B. weakened respiratory muscles
    C. hyperventilation
    D. decreased cough reflex

31. Nursing interventions to protect this patient from injury include all of the following   31.____
    EXCEPT

    A. avoiding restraints, sedatives or tranquilizers
    B. keeping bed high above the floor
    C. maintaining a quiet environment
    D. speaking in low, calm, soothing tone

32. Which of the following are symptoms of oxygen narcosis?   32.____

    A. Decreased respiratory rate and depth
    B. Flushing of skin
    C. Headache and confusion progressing to coma
    D. All of the above

33. Education of the patient so that he can live as actively as possible within the limitations of   33.____
    the disease includes

    A. cough suppression techniques
    B. stressing the need for intense daily exercise
    C. postural drainage
    D. all of the above

Questions 34-35.

DIRECTIONS: Questions 34 and 35 are to be answered on the basis of the following informa-
              tion.

    An 18-year-old boy has nasal discharge, sneezing, fever, and watery eyes for the last
four days. A common cold is diagnosed.

34. Nursing interventions to educate the patient for self-management include all of the following EXCEPT   34.____

    A. resting to conserve energy for the body to use in fighting the infection
    B. decreasing fluid intake to help liquefy secretions
    C. using a vaporizer to soothe mucous membranes and liquefy secretions
    D. blowing nose by opening the mouth slightly and blowing through both nostrils to equalize pressure

35. Nursing instructions to the above patient for the control of spread of the disease include   35.____

    A. covering mouth when sneezing or coughing
    B. properly disposing of used tissues
    C. avoiding crowded areas
    D. all of the above

_____

KEY (CORRECT ANSWERS)

1.	B		16.	A
2.	B		17.	B
3.	A		18.	B
4.	A		19.	B
5.	C		20.	C
6.	B		21.	A
7.	B		22.	A
8.	D		23.	C
9.	C		24.	C
10.	A		25.	B
11.	B		26.	D
12.	C		27.	B
13.	B		28.	A
14.	D		29.	C
15.	A		30.	C

31.	B
32.	D
33.	C
34.	B
35.	D

_____

TEST 2

DIRECTIONS: Each question or incomplete statement is followed by several suggested answers or completions. Select the one that BEST answers the question or completes the statement. *PRINT THE LETTER OF THE CORRECT ANSWER IN THE SPACE AT THE RIGHT.*

1. A 55-year-old patient is admitted with impaired peripheral arterial circulation. The nurse should tell the patient to avoid or eliminate all of the following EXCEPT

    A. exposure to temperature extremes   B. excessive exercise
    C. loose clothing   D. tobacco

1.____

2. Nursing advice for the modification of diet in the above patient includes all of the following EXCEPT

    A. high sodium
    B. low cholesterol
    C. moderate fat
    D. reduced calories if patient is obese

2.____

3. Nursing intervention to protect a patient with thrombophelibitis from dislodgement of the thrombus include all of the following EXCEPT

    A. maintaining bed rest for 7-10 days
    B. performing valsalva maneuver
    C. applying warm, moist packs to involved site
    D. advising patient not to rub legs

3.____

Questions 4-7.

DIRECTIONS: Questions 4 through 7 are to be answered on the basis of the following information.

A 30-year-old alcoholic male develops fever with cough; on auscultation rales are heard. An x-ray shows an area of consolidation.

4. Organisms involved in pneumonia include all of the following EXCEPT

    A. S. pneumonia   B. H. influenza
    C. compylobacter jejuni   D. moraxella catarrhalis

4.____

5. Nursing interventions to improve pulmonary ventilation include all of the following EXCEPT

    A. decreasing fluid intake   B. providing good oral hygiene
    C. discouraging antitussives   D. administering analgesics for chest pain

5.____

6. The nursing objective for keeping the patient free from atelactasis will be achieved by all of the following EXCEPT

    A. assessing patient status every 2-4 hours   B. reducing anxiety
    C. positioning patient on affected side   D. checking pulse rate

6.____

7. Nursing instructions for the self-care of this patient after discharge include   7.____

    A. 20 minutes of cardiovascular exercise 3 times per week
    B. pneumococcal vaccine if a high-risk patient
    C. oxygen therapy
    D. all of the above

Questions 8-13.

DIRECTIONS: Questions 8 through 13 are to be answered on the basis of the following information.

    A 50-year-old black male develops increasing cough with sputum production, weight loss, hemoptysis, and fatigue. A chest x-ray shows calcified intrathoracic lymph nodes and infiltrates in the posterior segment of upper lobes.

8. The MOST likely diagnosis is   8.____

    A. bronchiatasis   B. tuberculosis
    C. asthma   D. none of the above

9. A nursing evaluation of predisposing factors for tuberculosis does NOT include   9.____

    A. alcoholism
    B. overcrowded, poorly ventilated living conditions
    C. debilitating diseases
    D. immunosuppressive conditions

10. Nursing interventions to arrest active tuberculosis do NOT include   10.____

    A. administering antituberculous drugs as ordered
    B. surgical removal of tuberculous tissue
    C. providing adequate rest
    D. instituting a nutritionally adequate diet

11. Nursing implementations for the patient to cope with the disease do NOT include   11.____

    A. encouraging suppression of fears, concerns or questions
    B. advising patient of social stigma associated with tuberculosis
    C. spending time talking with the patient
    D. all of the above

12. Nursing interventions to ensure that the patient will practice health habits that prevent   12.____
reactivation of infection include all of the following EXCEPT stressing the

    A. importance of follow-up care
    B. need to swallow, rather than spit up, sputum
    C. importance of physical activity
    D. use of isolation techniques if necessary

13. Certain individuals are at high risk for the development of significant symptomatic tuber-   13.____
culosis and should be offered chemoprophylaxis.
High risk groups do NOT include

    A. adolescents between 13-21 years of age
    B. individuals who live in the same house or come in close contact with an infected or
        contagious patient
    C. individuals in which a -VE skin test turns +VE
    D. individuals with a positive skin test who receive corticosteroid therapy

14. A woman develops chills, headache, sneezing, nasal discharge, and obstruction. A com-   14.____
mon cold is diagnosed. Nursing instructions in this case include all of the following
EXCEPT

    A. observing careful handwashing techniques to avoid person-to-person spread of
        virus-contaminated secretions
    B. maximizing alcohol intake
    C. employing humidity measures indoors during winter months
    D. avoiding irritating substances such as smoke, chemicals, dust, and sprays

15. A 45-year-old patient with COPD develops increasing dyspnea, fatigue, and peripheral   15.____
edema. An x-ray shows right heart enlargement.
The MOST likely diagnosis is

    A. chronic bronchitis   B. cor pulmonale
    C. tuberculosis   D. lung abscess

16. Nursing interventions to monitor the above patient and his response to therapy include all   16.____
of the following EXCEPT

    A. watching for alterations in electrolyte levels, especially potassium
    B. employing ECG monitoring to detect dysrhythmia
    C. encouraging physical activity
    D. restricting sodium intake if there is evidence of fluid retention

17. Nursing interventions to improve ventilation and correct hypoxemia in a patient with cor   17.____
pulmonale include all of the following EXCEPT

    A. monitoring arterial blood gas values
    B. using continuous high-flow oxygen
    C. avoiding CNS depressants
    D. combatting respiratory infections

18. To promote muscle relaxation and to slow the respiratory rate, breathing exercises are   18.____
offered to a number of patients.
The nurse's role involves all of the following EXCEPT

    A. advising the patient to breathe slowly and rhythmically in a relaxed manner to per-
        mit complete exhalation and emptying of lungs
    B. advising patient to inhale through the mouth
    C. scheduling breathing exercise sessions 2-4 times daily
    D. discontinuing breathing exercises if shortness of breath occurs

19. The nurse's role in a patient undergoing postural drainage includes 19.____
    A. giving bronchodilator aerosol medications, if ordered, before the procedure
    B. instructing the patient to suppress a cough when position is changed
    C. suctioning the drainage tube during the procedure
    D. all of the above

20. The goal of using intermittent positive pressure breathing (IPPB) in a patient with respira- 20.____
tory failure includes
    A. delivering aerosols that mobilize secretions and promote coughing
    B. assisting in ventilation in order to decrease the work of breathing
    C. preventing atelectasis
    D. all of the above

Questions 21-25.

DIRECTIONS: Questions 21 through 25 are to be answered on the basis of the following information.

A 65-year-old CVA patient aspirates fluid and develops progressive tachypnea and dyspnea. Pulmonary function and blood gas studies show increased minute ventilation, decreased
lung volume, and acute respiratory alkalosis. An x-ray shows patchy diffuse bilateral fluffy
infiltrates.

21. The MOST likely diagnosis is 21.____
    A. adult respiratory distress syndrome   B. reactivated tuberculosis
    C. pneumonia   D. none of the above

22. For the purpose of mechanical ventilation, a tracheotomy is done on this patient. 22.____
Nursing interventions to keep a patent airway include all of the following EXCEPT
    A. recording respiratory rate and characteristics every 4 hours
    B. elevating the foot end of the bed
    C. providing humidification
    D. keeping obstructive material such as sheets or cotton away from the stoma

23. Nursing interventions to keep this patient free from infection do NOT include 23.____
    A. inspecting skin around stoma for signs of inflammation every 2-4 hours initially
    B. washing the skin around the stoma with soap and water every morning
    C. changing the external dressing and ties when wet or soiled
    D. applying povidone-iodine ointment around the stoma and covering with a sterile
       dressing

24. Nursing interventions to aid a patient in establishing an effective communication method 24.____
do NOT usually include
    A. providing pad and pencil or erasable slate for writing
    B. arranging signal for bells or buzzers
    C. working out an alternative method of communication for common needs
    D. teaching the patient ASL (American sign language)

25. Nursing interventions to decrease patient anxiety include   25.____

    A. explaining the process to the patient and significant others carefully
    B. preventing the patient from seeing the procedure or equipment
    C. allowing the patient to read a surgical description of tracheotomy techniques
    D. all of the above

26. Application of nursing processes to a patient at high risk for aspiration during a broncho-   26.____
scopy includes

    A. positioning the patient in a flat or semi-Fowler's side lying position
    B. instructing the patient to let saliva drain out of the corner of the mouth into a basin or tissue
    C. keeping patient NPO until the swallow or cough reflex returns
    D. all of the above

27. A 45-year-old male is on transtracheal oxygen therapy after severe trauma to the chest.   27.____
The nurse educating the patient for self-management should advise him to immediately report all of the following signs or symptoms EXCEPT

    A. a cough unrelieved by cough suppressant
    B. decreased sputum production
    C. cyanosis of the lips or nail beds
    D. edema of the face or neck

28. Pneumonectomy is the surgical removal of an entire lung. Indications for pneumonec-   28.____
tomy include all of the following EXCEPT

    A. bronchogenic carcinoma
    B. atypical pneumonia
    C. bronchiectasis
    D. extensive unilateral tuberculosis

29. Nursing guidelines to aid in educating a patient for self-management after a pneumonec-   29.____
tomy include

    A. eliminating all contact with smoke
    B. performing breathing, cardiovascular, and upper body exercises for 45 minutes every day
    C. avoiding heavy lifting
    D. all of the above

30. A 25-year-old man has a sudden onset of a sore throat accompanied by chills and high   30.____
grade fever. He also has some difficulty in swallowing. The patient is diagnosed with
acute pharyngitis.
Nursing instructions to this patient include all of the following EXCEPT:

    A. Drink 2000-3000 ml of fluid per day
    B. Drink citrus juices
    C. Consume cool, clear fluids or ice to soothe the throat during the acute stage of dis-
ease
    D. Adjust diet from clear liquids to full liquids to a pureed or soft diet, depending on individual tolerance

31. Nursing advice to a patient who has undergone a tonsillectomy for peritonsillar abscess   31.____
(quincy) includes all of the following EXCEPT

   A. adding soft food to the diet as tolerated
   B. resting in bed or on a couch for 24 hours after the operation and then gradually
resume full activity
   C. adding foods such as salads and orange juice to the diet
   D. reporting any heavy bleeding or a temperature greater than 100.4° F

32. A 49-year-old patient with arterial hypertension comes to the emergency room with   32.____
epistaxis.
Nursing interventions should include

   A. loosening clothing around the neck to prevent pressure on the carotid arteries
   B. assisting the patient to a prone position
   C. performing cardiac compressions
   D. all of the above

33. A patient with acute bronchitis is being discharged. Nursing instructions for the preven-   33.____
tion of recurrent infection include

   A. maintaining a cool environment, 62-68°
   B. avoiding exposure to environmental irritants like smoke and air pollutants
   C. eating a high carbohydrate-high fiber diet
   D. all of the above

34. A patient with pneumonia is being discharged.   34.____
Nursing instructions to increase metabolic demands secondary to infection and to
increase respiratory rate include all of the following EXCEPT

   A. consuming at least 1500 calories daily
   B. aiming for a positive nitrogen balance to replete body tissue
   C. ensuring a diet rich in fats
   D. a liquid or blenderized diet may be better tolerated in the beginning

35. Nursing advice to a patient with lung cancer for decreasing risks of respiratory infection   35.____
includes

   A. maintain good oral hygiene
   B. avoid crowds
   C. drink at least 10 glasses of liquid daily
   D. all of the above

KEY (CORRECT ANSWERS)

1.	C		16.	C
2.	A		17.	B
3.	B		18.	B
4.	C		19.	A
5.	A		20.	D
6.	C		21.	A
7.	B		22.	B
8.	B		23.	B
9.	A		24.	C
10.	B		25.	A
11.	A		26.	D
12.	B		27.	B
13.	A		28.	B
14.	B		29.	C
15.	B		30.	B

31.	C
32.	A
33.	B
34.	C
35.	D

EXAMINATION SECTION
TEST 1

DIRECTIONS: Each question or incomplete statement is followed by several suggested answers or completions. Select the one that BEST answers the question or completes the statement. *PRINT THE LETTER OF THE CORRECT ANSWER IN THE SPACE AT THE RIGHT.*

1. Nursing interventions to make a patient understand the importance of periodic examinations in reproductive health maintenance include   1.____

    A. explaining the need for papanicolaou (PAP) smears
    B. explaining the importance of regular breast self-examination
    C. providing supplemental reading materials to increase patient's knowledge
    D. all of the above

2. Health education recommendations to reduce the risk of osteoporosis in adult women include all of the following EXCEPT   2.____

    A. eating a balanced diet to ensure adequate vitamin and mineral intake
    B. increasing fats and multiple phosphorus supplements
    C. increasing daily food sources of calcium
    D. exercising regularly to strengthen bones

Questions 3-5.

DIRECTIONS: Questions 3 through 5 are to be answered on the basis of the following information.

    A 28-year-old black woman presents with hypermenorrhea and mild lower abdominal pain. She also complains of urinary frequency and constipation.

3. The MOST likely diagnosis is   3.____

    A. myomata uteri   B. pelvic inflammatory disease
    C. endometriosis   D. all of the above

4. Predisposing factors for the above condition include all of the following EXCEPT   4.____

    A. infertility   B. hormone usage
    C. diabetes mellitus   D. age

5. Nursing interventions to keep the patient free from problems during conservative management of this condition include   5.____

    A. supporting the patient's decision for immediate pregnancy
    B. monitoring for increased severity of symptoms
    C. discouraging hormone usage
    D. all of the above

6. Predisposing factors for vaginal wall changes, associated with childbearing or aging, include all of the following EXCEPT   6.____

    A. hirsutism
    B. multiparity
    C. inappropriate bearing down during labor
    D. congenital weakness

7. As a result of reproduction, all of the following changes are expected in the uterus   7._____
   EXCEPT

   A. increase in length, width, and depth
   B. shape changes from oval to globular
   C. weight increases from 60-1000 g.
   D. distension out of pelvis at twelfth week

8. All of the following statements about changes in the vagina during pregnancy are true   8._____
   EXCEPT:

   A. Increased vascularity
   B. Thinning of the mucosa
   C. Loosening of connective tissue
   D. Increased vaginal discharge without signs of itching or burning

9. All of the following are subjective signs and symptoms of pregnancy EXCEPT   9._____

   A. quickening
   B. Hegar's sign
   C. Goodell's sign
   D. Braxton-Hicks contractions

10. Which of the following is NOT a function of the placenta?   10._____

   A. Hormone secretion from the early weeks of pregnancy
   B. A barrier to some substances and organisms
   C. Fluid and gas transport
   D. Cushioning the fetus inside placental membranes

11. Nursing goals of health promotion through anticipatory guidance can be achieved by all   11._____
    of the following EXCEPT

   A. telling patients to expect a decreased need for sleep during pregnancy
   B. advising patients to continue their usual exercise regimen
   C. recommending comfortable, nonrestricting maternity clothing, a well-fitting bra, and
      low-heeled supportive shoes
   D. advising patients to stop or reduce cigarette consumption

12. In the health maintenance program of a pregnant woman, nursing interventions for relief   12._____
    of common discomforts include all of the following EXCEPT

   A. eating dry crackers or toast before slowly arising
   B. eating greasy, highly seasoned foods at one meal per day
   C. drinking adequate fluids between meals
   D. eating a protein snack at bedtime

13. Nursing instructions for avoiding varicose veins would be to   13._____

   A. elevate legs frequently when sitting or lying down in bed
   B. avoid sitting or standing for prolonged periods or crossing legs at the knees
   C. avoid tight or constricting hosiery or garters
   D. all of the above

14. Which of the following are NOT nutritional risk factors at the early stages of pregnancy?   14.____

    A. Mild obesity
    B. Frequent pregnancies and adolescence
    C. Vegetarian diet
    D. Smoking, drug addiction, or alcoholism

15. Predisposing factors for ectopic pregnancies include all of the following EXCEPT   15.____

    A. repeated pregnancies
    B. pelvic inflammatory disease (PID)
    C. puerperal and postabortal sepsis
    D. prolonged use of IUD

16. Nursing interventions for a patient with an ectopic pregnancy do NOT include   16.____

    A. monitoring vital signs and continually assessing for shock
    B. preparing client for surgery
    C. supporting the grieving process
    D. counseling patient on possible demise of fetus

17. A 37-year-old primipara is diagnosed with pregnancy-induced hypertension. She has no   17.____
    prior history of hypertension.
    Nursing interventions in this case include

    A. detecting preeclampsia through early and regular antepartal care
    B. instructing the patient to weigh herself daily
    C. monitoring IRO, blood pressure, weight, urine for protein, FHR for hospitalized
       patients
    D. all of the above

18. Nursing interventions to keep a hypertensive patient free from physical injury in the event   18.____
    of a seizure do NOT include

    A. maintaining a patent airway
    B. utilizing full body restraints
    C. monitoring for signs of abruptio placentae
    D. noting nature, onset, and progression of seizure

19. A 29-year-old female at the end of her first trimester of pregnancy is diagnosed having a   19.____
    valvular heart defect. Nursing interventions to prevent anemia and cardiac decompensa-
    tion include

    A. encouraging early and more frequent antepartal care; monitoring vital signs, fetal
       heart rate, and weight
    B. teaching proper nutrition with adequate iron intake to prevent anemia
    C. emphasizing the need for additional rest and stress reduction
    D. all of the above

20. In the postpartum period, nursing interventions in the same patient consist of all of the following EXCEPT   20.____

    A. assessing for signs of hemorrhage
    B. assessing for congestive cardiac failure
    C. administering ergonovine and other oxytocins
    D. assessing for thromboembolism

21. A 17-year-old female has hyperemesis gravidarum.   21.____
Nursing interventions should include

    A. administering parenteral fluids
    B. promoting a quiet environment
    C. providing frequent, small meals when oral feeding is tolerated
    D. all of the above

22. A 26-year-old black female took clomophine for the induction of ovulation. She is now   22.____
pregnant with twins.
Nursing interventions for this patient include all of the following EXCEPT

    A. advising rest in the right lateral position to provide oxygenation for the fetal/placental unit
    B. monitoring fetal heart rate carefully for fetal distress
    C. promoting a balanced diet, with adequate protein, iron, and vitamin supplements
    D. preparing for vaginal delivery unless complications arise

23. All of the following signs and symptoms favor a diagnosis of *true* labor EXCEPT   23.____

    A. contractions increasing progressively in strength, duration, and frequency
    B. discomfort felt in lower abdomen and groin
    C. increasing effacement and dilatation of cervix
    D. regular pattern not relieved by walking

24. Physiological alterations occurring during labor do NOT include   24.____

    A. cervical dilatation up to 10 cm
    B. expulsion of the umbilical cord
    C. effacement, thinning, shortening, and obliteration of cervix
    D. separation of upper and lower uterine segments

25. Nursing interventions to ensure that a patient will remain stable during the recovery   25.____
period following delivery include

    A. taking vital signs every 15 minutes until stable
    B. having patient ambulatory within 30 minutes of delivery
    C. administration of analgesics
    D. all of the above

26. Nursing interventions checking pre-term labor and allowing the patient to carry the fetus   26.____
as close to term as possible include all of the following EXCEPT

    A. maintaining bed rest in the lateral recumbent position in a quiet environment
    B. administering a selected oxytocin agent
    C. maintaining adequate hydration through oral or parenteral intake
    D. providing emotional support

27. A forceps delivery is planned on a 29-year-old diabetic woman due to a suspected large   27._____
head obstruction. Nursing interventions to ensure that the patient and fetus will experience minimal trauma despite the delivery would NOT include

   A. providing the physician with selected forceps
   B. padding the forceps with sterile gauze
   C. monitoring fetal heart rate continuously during the procedure
   D. assessing the newborn for forceps bruises and facial paralysis

28. All of the following are indications for a cesarean birth EXCEPT   28._____

   A. a diabetic mother
   B. cephalopelvic disproportion
   C. a prolapsed cord
   D. active herpes lesions

29. Nursing interventions after a cesarean birth do NOT include   29._____

   A. assessing for signs and symptoms of hemorrhage
   B. providing assistance as necessary during mother-infant interactions
   C. stressing the importance of post-cesarean delivery exercises
   D. monitoring maternal-fetal status

30. Nursing interventions in a case of postpartal hemorrhage include all of the following   30._____
EXCEPT

   A. massaging boggy fundus gently but firmly
   B. administering oxytocic agents in the fourth stage of labor
   C. discouraging frequent voiding
   D. replacing fluid and blood as ordered

_____

KEY (CORRECT ANSWERS)

1.	D		16.	D
2.	B		17.	D
3.	A		18.	B
4.	C		19.	D
5.	D		20.	C
6.	A		21.	D
7.	B		22.	A
8.	B		23.	B
9.	A		24.	B
10.	D		25.	A
11.	A		26.	B
12.	B		27.	B
13.	D		28.	A
14.	A		29.	C
15.	A		30.	C

TEST 2

Questions 1-4.

DIRECTIONS: Questions 1 through 4 are to be answered on the basis of the following information.

A 27-year-old black female has 101° F fever on the third day after delivering an 8 lb. boy. She has had three other deliveries without complications. This time she has a history of prolonged labor after the rupture of membranes.

1. Bacterial organisms responsible for this condition include all of the following EXCEPT   1.____

   A. a mixed aerobic-anaerobic infection
   B. E. coli
   C. compylobacter
   D. streptococcus hemolyticus

2. Predisposing conditions for this disorder do NOT include   2.____

   A. soft tissue trauma and/or hemorrhage
   B. retention of placental fragments
   C. multiparity
   D. debilitating antepartal conditions

3. Nursing interventions in the management of this patient include   3.____

   A. encouraging a semi-Fowler's position to facilitate lochia drainage
   B. reinforcing perineal hygiene techniques
   C. providing comfort measures, i.e., sitz baths, to promote perineal healing
   D. all of the above

4. If the puerperal fever is due to mastitis, nursing interventions should include all of the following EXCEPT   4.____

   A. promoting comfort by suggesting a supportive bra
   B. terminating lactation in breastfeeding mothers
   C. encouraging good handwashing and breast hygiene
   D. preparing the patient for incision and drainage of abscess if necessary

5. Advanced gestational age and placental insufficiency could cause all of the following EXCEPT   5.____

   A. a thick, short newborn
   B. dry, parchment-like skin
   C. a decreased or absent vernix
   D. meconium staining of amniotic fluid

6. After the 34th week of gestation, a stress test or contraction stress test is used to evalu-   6._____
   ate the ability of the fetus to withstand the stress of uterine contractions as would occur
   during labor.
   Nursing interventions in the performance of this test include all of the following
   EXCEPT

   A. placing the woman in a semi-Fowler's or side lying position
   B. advising the woman to hold her urine prior to the test
   C. obtaining a 30 minute strip of the fetal heart rate and uterine activity for baseline
      data
   D. administering a diluted oxytocin via an infusion pump

7. Contraindications for an oxytocin challenge or stress test include all of the following   7._____
   EXCEPT

   A. a previous cesarean birth
   B. third trimester bleeding
   C. a non-reactive nonstress test
   D. all of the above

8. Metabolic screening tests should be done for all of the following pathological conditions   8._____
   EXCEPT

   A. phenylketonuria   B. scurvy
   C. sickle cell anemia   D. hypothyroidism

Questions 9-10.

DIRECTIONS: Questions 9 and 10 are to be answered on the basis of the following informa-
              tion.

   A 22-year-old white female at 16 weeks of gestation comes to the emergency room with
persistent bleeding. On examination, her uterus is large for gestational age. Hydatiform mole
is diagnosed based on laboratory results.

9. Nursing interventions to ensure adequate fluid status of the patient would NOT include   9._____

   A. having the patient drink 1000 cc of fluid every two hours
   B. establishing and maintaining an IV line with a large needle
   C. assessing maternal vital signs and evaluating bleeding
   D. typing and screening the blood and having 2-4 units of whole blood available

10. In the health education plan of this patient, all of the following should be advised   10._____
    EXCEPT

   A. the need for follow-up care and the importance of continuing the follow-up care
   B. avoiding pregnancy for a minimum of 1 month
   C. biweekly measurement of chorionic gonadotropin levels
   D. a rise in chorionic gonadotropin levels or plateau requires further treatment

Questions 11-16.

DIRECTIONS: Questions 11 through 16 are to be answered on the basis of the following information.

A 35-year-old white female has a hard, discharging lump on the upper outer side of her
right breast. After a thorough examination and laboratory work-up, carcinoma of the breast is
diagnosed.

11.   Major predisposing factors for carcinoma of the breast include all of the following   11.____
EXCEPT

    A.   late menarche and early menopause
    B.   a family history of breast cancer on the maternal side
    C.   uterine cancer
    D.   chronic irritation; fibrocystic disease

12.   Nursing guidelines in preparing this patient for surgery do NOT include   12.____

    A.   having patient sign an organ donor card
    B.   exploring patient's expectations of what the surgical site will look like
    C.   discussing the possibility of reconstructive surgery
    D.   allaying anxiety and fear

13.   Nursing interventions to ensure that the patient will regain joint and arm movement on   13.____
the side of the surgery include

    A.   positioning the arm on the operative side on a pillow to decrease incidence of
lymphedema
    B.   teaching exercises at the appropriate time to prevent contracture of the shoulder
and to promote lymphatic flow
    C.   having patient use arm and hand for daily activities (e.g., brushing hair)
    D.   all of the above

14.   Nursing interventions to explain incision care and the choice of available prostheses   14.____
include all of the following EXCEPT

    A.   encouraging the patient to look at the incision
    B.   upon discharge having patient wear her own bra with cotton padding
    C.   teaching patient not to wash the incision with soap and water
    D.   discussing with the patient plans for obtaining a permanent prosthesis

15.   Nursing education of the patient to describe lymphedema and state ways to prevent it   15.____
includes all of the following EXCEPT

    A.   suggesting patient elevate arm throughout the day
    B.   advising patient to wear a constrictive bandage around her arm
    C.   suggesting that the patient decrease sodium and fluid intake
    D.   teaching the patient to sleep with arm elevated on a pillow

16. Of the following precautions, the one which a nurse should NOT encourage to prevent   16.____
infections in a mastectomy patient is

    A. not to shave axilla on the affected side and attend to any small cut or scrape imme-
diately
    B. using only electrolysis to depillate the axilla on the affected side
    C. avoiding blood pressure measurements, injections, and blood drawing on the
affected side
    D. avoiding carrying heavy objects with affected arm

Questions 17-20.

DIRECTIONS: Questions 17 through 20 are to be answered on the basis of the following information.

A 62-year-old black singer comes to the emergency room with complaints of hoarseness
and dyspnea. A diagnostic work-up of the patient is done, and he is diagnosed with glottic
(vocal cords) cancer.

17. Risk factors for laryngeal cancer include all of the following EXCEPT   17.____

    A. cocaine abuse
    B. familial predisposition
    C. excessive alcohol intake and smoking
    D. vocal abuse

18. Post-operatively, nursing interventions to maintain adequate respiratory function include   18.____
all of the following EXCEPT

    A. frequent assessment for patency of airway and rate and depth of respiration
    B. promoting drainage and facilitation by having the patient lie flat on bed
    C. administration of humidified oxygen
    D. frequent suction of tracheostomy

19. Nursing measures to ensure that the patient will have satisfactory post-operative com-   19.____
munication abilities do NOT include

    A. using communications measures decided upon pre-operatively
    B. encouraging the patient to use his voice as soon as possible
    C. staying with the patient as often as possible
    D. explaining to the patient how to summon a nurse and responding promptly when
called

20. In discharge planning for this patient, the nurse should advise him to   20.____

    A. always keep the stoma covered for hygienic management of secretions
    B. avoid cold air
    C. expect some loss of smell and impairment of taste sensation
    D. all of the above

21. A prostatectomy has been done on a 65-year-old patient who was admitted to the floor   21.____
    with complaints of frequency, urgency, and some incontinence.
    Nursing interventions to keep a clean, intact incision do NOT include

    A. washing the incision with soap and water twice a day
    B. no insertion of thermometers or tubes
    C. giving sitz baths after drains are removed
    D. maintaining patency of foley catheter

22. Nursing interventions to ensure that the patient will regain perineal muscle tone and uri-   22.____
    nary continence include all of the following EXCEPT

    A. teaching pubo-coccygeal exercises
    B. instituting exercises immediately after operation
    C. encouraging the patient to perform exercises hourly
    D. reassuring the patient that some urinary control can be obtained

23. Of the following, the BEST initial means of detecting abnormal breast masses is by   23.____

    A. annual mammography
    B. biopsy
    C. breast self-examination
    D. annual gynecologic examinations

24. In a patient receiving radiation therapy, nutritional planning should include   24.____

    A. a low-residue diet   B. sodium restriction
    C. a high fiber diet   D. all of the above

25. Abnormal cellular growths which are generally benign do NOT include   25.____

    A. hydatidiform mole   B. fibroid tumors
    C. epitheliomas   D. lipomas

KEY (CORRECT ANSWERS)

1.	C	11.	A
2.	C	12.	A
3.	D	13.	D
4.	B	14.	C
5.	A	15.	B
6.	B	16.	B
7.	C	17.	A
8.	B	18.	B
9.	A	19.	B
10.	B	20.	D

21.	A
22.	B
23.	C
24.	A
25.	C

EXAMINATION SECTION
TEST 1

DIRECTIONS: Each question or incomplete statement is followed by several suggested answers or completions. Select the one that BEST answers the question or completes the statement. *PRINT THE LETTER OF THE CORRECT ANSWER IN THE SPACE AT THE RIGHT.*

1. A patient is admitted to the hospital with a diagnosis of Adams-Stokes syndrome. His symptoms will MOST likely include   1.____

   A. slurred speech and flushing
   B. vertigo and nausea
   C. low ventricular rate and syncope
   D. blurred vision

2. A client complains of frequent leg cramps after delivering twins. A nurse should suspect   2.____

   A. hypocalcemia   B. hypokalemia
   C. hypercalcemia   D. hyperkalemia

3. A client has been diagnosed with basal cell carcinoma. The nurse's questioning of the client should focus on the client's   3.____

   A. smoking history
   B. family history of cancer
   C. diet
   D. exposure to ultraviolet radiation

4. The MOST common side effect associated with the use of IUDs is   4.____

   A. ectopic pregnancy   B. missed periods
   C. uterine rupture   D. heavy menstrual flow

5. A client suffers a complete pneumothorax, and consequently a mediastinal shift. The client's MOST immediate risk is   5.____

   A. rupture of the pericardium
   B. decreased filling of the right heart
   C. infection of the subpleural lining
   D. increased volume in the unaffected lung

6. Generally, as a patient's red blood cell count *increases*, the   6.____

   A. patient's immunity *decreases*
   B. patient's hematocrit *decreases*
   C. blood viscosity *increases*
   D. blood pH *increases*

7. A client receiving anticoagulants should be observed for   7.____

   A. epistaxis   B. chest pain
   C. nausea   D. hemoptysis

8. A pregnant woman with _____ is MOST likely to experience abrupto placentae.   8.____

    A. hyperthyroidism
    B. cephalopelvic disproportion
    C. pregnancy-induced hypertension
    D. cardiac disease

9. What is the preferred treatment for malignant melanoma of the eye?   9.____

    A. Cryosurgery   B. Chemotherapy
    C. Enucleation   D. Radiation

10. While a pacemaker catheter is being inserted, a client's heart rate drops to 36. The nurse   10.____
should expect the physician to order

    A. Pronestyl   B. Atropine sulfate
    C. Lanoxin   D. Lidocaine

11. In the absence of pathology, a client's respiratory system is stimulated by   11.____

    A. carbon dioxide   B. sodium ions
    C. oxygen   D. lactic acid

12. Where should a nurse place the stethoscope when taking a client's apical pulse?   12.____

    A. In the fifth intercostal space, along the left mid-clavicular line
    B. Between the sixth and seventh ribs, at the left mid-axillary line
    C. Just to the left of the midpoint of the sternum
    D. Between the third and fourth ribs, to the left of the sternum

13. A client receiving vincristine as treatment for leukemia should be placed on a diet that is   13.____

    A. high in fluids, but low in residue
    B. high in both fluids and roughage
    C. low in fluids, with increased iron
    D. low in fat

14. The MOST significant causes of puerperal or postpartal infection are hemorrhage and   14.____

    A. anemia during pregnancy
    B. preeclampsia
    C. organisms present in the birth canal
    D. trauma during labor

15. A client is admitted to the hospital with carcinoma of the descending colon, with   15.____
metastases to the lymph nodes.
Which procedure would be performed?

    A. Colostomy   B. Colectomy
    C. Ileostomy   D. Cecostomy

16. Which of the following conditions is the clearest contraindication for the administration of   16.____
Librium?

    A. Hypotension   B. Muscle twitching
    C. Extreme drowsiness   D. Blurred vision

17. A client who is receiving aminophylline intravenously should be observed for   17.____

    A. decreased urinary output   B. hypotension
    C. auditory hallucinations   D. decreased pulse rate

18. What is the MOST common symptom of a rectrocele caused by overstretching of perineal supporting tissues during childbirth?   18.____

    A. A sensation of bearing down
    B. Recurrent urinary tract infections
    C. Urinary incontinence
    D. Sharp abdominal pain

19. Which of the following is an early manifestation of cancer of the cervix?   19.____

    A. A full-bladder manifestation
    B. A sensation of having a full stomach
    C. Bloody spotting after intercourse
    D. Malodorous discharge

20. A client with a long history of emphysema is now terminally ill with cancer of the stomach. Her plan of care includes modified postural drainage, a soft diet, and nebulizer treatments twice a day. She is weak, apathetic, and dyspneic.
The nursing care plan for this patient should give priority to   20.____

    A. posture and body mechanics
    B. intake and output
    C. comfort and hygiene
    D. diet and nutrition

21. A 60-year-old female.client is admitted to the hospital with a diagnosis of hypertension. She is placed on a cardiac monitor, and her serum potassium level is low. She is to receive intravenously 40 mEq potassium chloride in 750 ml of 5% dextrose in water. When observing the monitor pattern in order to obtain a baseline for the evaluation of the client's progress, what would be shown by the monitor pattern?   21.____

    A. Spiking of the ST segment
    B. Increased Q wave deflection
    C. Lowering of the T wave
    D. Shortened QRS complex

22. Following a thoracentesis, it is MOST important for a nurse to observe a client for   22.____

    A. shallow breathing   B. blurred vision
    C. spitting blood   D. increased breath sounds

23. During what period is prenatal growth MOST rapid?   23.____

    A. Implantation   B. 1st trimester
    C. 2nd trimester   D. 3rd trimester

24. A client receiving chemotherapy for cancer of the bone is at risk for mouth lesions. The   24.____
nurse should instruct the client to

   A. brush with foam-tipped applicators
   B. rinse the mouth frequently with undiluted antibacterial mouthwash
   C. brush three times a day with a toothbrush
   D. rinse the mouth frequently with hydrogen peroxide

25. A client on a cardiac monitor displays ventricular irritability. Which of the following should   25.____
the nurse prepare to administer?

   A. Heparin   B. Levophed
   C. Lidocaine   D. Lanoxin

_____

KEY (CORRECT ANSWERS)

1. C	11. A		
2. A	12. A		
3. D	13. B		
4. D	14. D		
5. B	15. A		
6. C	16. C		
7. A	17. B		
8. C	18. A		
9. C	19. C		
10. B	20. C		

21. C
22. C
23. D
24. A
25. C

_____

TEST 2

DIRECTIONS: Each question or incomplete statement is followed by several suggested answers or completions. Select the one that BEST answers the question or completes the statement. *PRINT THE LETTER OF THE CORRECT ANSWER IN THE SPACE AT THE RIGHT.*

1. The reason that emphysema decreases a patient's oxygen supply is because 1._____

   A. the patient is experiencing respiratory muscle paralysis
   B. there is a loss of aerating surface
   C. there is pleural effusion
   D. there are infectious obstructions in the lung and bronchii

2. A 27-year-old pregnant client claims to have weighed 100 pounds before pregnancy, and 2._____
   now, during her first trinester, she weighs 104 pounds. The client is concerned about
   regaining her figure after delivery, and expresses a wish to diet during pregnancy.
   The nurse should inform the client that

   A. since she is so small, dieting is often recommended to ease delivery
   B. dieting is often recommended to reduce the chances of stillbirth
   C. an inadequate food intake during pregnancy can result in a low birthweight infant
   D. an inadequate food intake during pregnancy can result in hypertension

3. A client has two Jackson-Pratt portable wound drainage systems in place after a modi- 3._____
   fied radical mastectomy.
   Which of the following would be involved in nursing care of these drains?

   A. Irrigating the drains with normal saline
   B. Leaving the drains open to the air to ensure maximum drainage
   C. Compressing the receptacles after emptying in order to maintain suction
   D. Attaching the tubes to straight drainage in order to monitor output

4. A nurse should measure a client's _____ before giving the client digoxin. 4._____

   A. radial pulse in both arms
   B. brachial pulse
   C. difference between apical and radial pulses
   D. apical pulse rate

5. When rotating tourniquets are used on a client with acute pulmonary edema, the tourni- 5._____
   quets are typically rotated every _____ minutes.

   A. 5   B. 15   C. 40   D. 60

6. A predisposing factor that causes morning sickness during the first trimester of preg- 6._____
   nancy is the mother's adaptation to increased levels of

   A. chorionic gonadotropin   B. progesterone
   C. estrogen   D. prolactin

7. Which of the following would MOST likely accompany atelectasis? 7._____

   A. Slow, deep respirations   B. A normal oral temperature
   C. Diminished breath sounds   D. A wheezy cough

8. A possible side effect of digitalis preparations is a depletion of   8._____

     A. sodium   B. phosphate   C. potassium   D. calcium

9. Which of the following would MOST likely be observed in a client with a cerebellar tumor?   9._____

     A. Execution of jerky, imprecise movements
     B. Inability to execute voluntary movements
     C. Unconsciousness
     D. Absent knee-jerk and other reflexes

10. A pregnant client with heart disease presents anemia with a hemoglobin level of 7.6 g. The client is at a high risk for   10._____

     A. atrial fibrillation   B. cardiac compensation
     C. cardiac failure   D. heart block

11. The radioisotope cesium-137 is commonly used in brachytherapy for each of the following EXCEPT _____ cancer.   11._____

     A. intracavitary uterine
     B. interstitial breast
     C. intracavitary cervical
     D. interstitial head and neck

12. A 58-year-old client is admitted to the hospital with severe dyspnea, and is expectorating blood. Cancer of the lung is suspected, and the client is scheduled for a bronchoscopy. If the client develops pleural effusion, it is MOST likely the result of   12._____

     A. low fluid intake
     B. shallow respiration
     C. enlargement of cancerous lesions
     D. irritation from the bronchoscopy

13. Which of the following would NOT typically be used to manage immune-mediated anemia that results from chronic lymphocytic leukemia?   13._____

     A. Allopurinol   B. Splenectomy
     C. IV gamma globulin   D. Prednisone

14. The ovum is believed to remain viable for _____ hours after ovulation.   14._____

     A. 1-4   B. 10-24   C. 24-36   D. 36-72

15. A client states that she experiences anginal pain after periods of activity. The nurse should suspect   15._____

     A. coronary thrombosis   B. arrhythmia
     C. mitral insufficiency   D. myocardial ischemia

16. Which of the following is involved in caring for a client following a craniotomy?   16._____

     A. Reporting yellow drainage on dressing immediately
     B. Administering sedatives at the first signs of irritability
     C. Encouraging deep coughing
     D. Taking only axillary temperatures

17. Which of the following is a precaution that must be taken against retrolental fibroplasia when caring for preterm infants?

17.____

   A. Maintain a high concentration of oxygen (above 70%) and high humidity
   B. Use phototherapy to prevent jaundice and retinopathy
   C. Carefully control temperature and humidity
   D. Keep oxygen at less than 40% concentration

18. The MOST common complication of chronic asthma is

18.____

   A. pneumothorax   B. atelectasis
   C. pulmonary embolism   D. emphysema

19. A nursing assessment of a client reveals pulmonary edema, MOST likely, this condition will be associated with

19.____

   A. pulmonary valve stenosis
   B. severe arteriosclerosis of the tricuspid valve
   C. mitral stenosis
   D. incomplete closure of the tricuspid valve

20. A physician orders that a client receive an intravenous digitalis preparation. Which of the following preparations would be given to the client?

20.____

   A. Deslanode   B. Digitalis leaf
   C. Digoxin   D. Gitalin

21. A nurse notes a prolapsed cord in a client in labor. The MOST effective position for this client would be

21.____

   A. Trendlenburg   B. Sims'
   C. half-Fowler's   D. prone

22. A client whose platelet count is very low should have her urine checked for the presence of

22.____

   A. lymphocytes   B. casts
   C. erythrocytes   D. leukocytes

23. Which of the following diagnosis categories would be prioritized first for treatment?

23.____

   A. Penetrating abdominal wound
   B. fractured tibia
   C. Head injury
   D. Ventricular fibrillation

24. A laboratory report showing acid-fast rods in a client's sputum would indicate the presence of

24.____

   A. mycobacterium tuberculosis
   B. bordatella pertussis
   C. influenza virus
   D. diphtheria bacillus

25. When instructing a client about the use of nitroglycerin tablets, the client should be informed that the tablets have probably lost their potency when

    A. pain occurs even after taking the tablet
    B. the client experiences increased facial flushing
    C. there is no tingling sensation accompanying the placement of the tablet under the tongue
    D. the onset of relief is delayed

25.____

KEY (CORRECT ANSWERS)

1.	B		11.	B
2.	C		12.	C
3.	C		13.	A
4.	D		14.	C
5.	B		15.	D
6.	A		16.	A
7.	C		17.	D
8.	C		18.	D
9.	A		19.	C
10.	C		20.	A

21.	A
22.	C
23.	D
24.	A
25.	C

TEST 3

DIRECTIONS: Each question or incomplete statement is followed by several suggested answers or completions. Select the one that BEST answers the question or completes the statement. *PRINT THE LETTER OF THE CORRECT ANSWER IN THE SPACE AT THE EIGHT.*

1. A client diagnosed with metastatic melanoma should be assessed for the presence of   1.____
    A. lymphadenopathy   B. sweating palms
    C. Nikolsky's sign   D. oily skin

2. If a nurse observes asymmetrical gluteal folds on a newborn infant, what is the MOST likely cause?   2.____
    A. Tissue necrosis due to uneven pressure
    B. Damage to the peripheral nervous system
    C. A dislocated hip
    D. An inguinal hernia

3. After being admitted to the emergency room, a client is diagnosed with a spontaneous pneumothorax. The client's assessment interview reveals that she has a history of emphysema. Later, the client becomes extremely drowsy, and her pulse and respirations increase.   3.____
    The MOST likely situation is
    A. elevated PO_2 B. hypokalemia
    C. respiratory alkalosis   D. hypercapnia

4. What is the chief function of progesterone?   4.____
    A. Developing female reproductive organs
    B. Preparing the uterus for receiving a fertilized ovum
    C. Stimulating follicles to ovulate
    D. Establishing secondary male sex characteristics

5. A client is diagnosed with acute lymphocytic leukemia. A nurse would commonly observe each of the following EXCEPT   5.____
    A. pallor   B. marked jaundice
    C. enlarged lymph nodes   D. multiple bruises

6. Which of the following molecules is/are capable of passing through the capillary endothelium?   6.____
    A. Plasma proteins   B. O_2 and water
    C. Ions   D. Glucose and CO_2

7. A client would receive isoproterenol in order to   7.____
    A. alleviate hypertension
    B. relax bronchial spasm
    C. increase bronchial secretions
    D. increase heart volume

8. Which of the following nursing recommendations may help a pregnant client overcome morning sickness?

    A. Taking a prescribed antiemetic
    B. Eating nothing until the nausea subsides
    C. Eating dry toast before getting out of bed in the morning
    D. Taking an antacid before bedtime

9. Before a client undergoes a surgical procedure to remove a carcinoma of the colon, the nurse would administer neoriycin sulfate in order to

    A. decrease the incidence of secondary infection
    B. destroy intestinal bacteria
    C. increase the production of vitamin E
    D. decrease the possibility of postoperative UTI

10. A likely effect of whole-body irradiation treatment for a client with Hodgkin's disease is

    A. *increased* tendency for fractures
    B. *decreased* number of erythrocytes
    C. *increased* immunity to infections
    D. *increased* blood viscosity

11. For what reason is chemotherapy delayed for a period of about 2 weeks following a radical mastectomy?

    A. The treatment may increase edema in areas near the incision by blocking lymph channels.
    B. It may cause vomiting, which would endanger the integrity of the incision area.
    C. It may decrease red blood cell production resulting in anemia.
    D. It may delay healing and interfere with cell growth.

12. The MOST common indication for cesarean delivery is

    A. jaundice
    B. vaginal atony
    C. cephalopelvic disproportion
    D. primary uterine inertia

13. Which of the following actions should be taken by a client on bed rest to prevent a pulmonary embolus?

    A. Periodically moving the legs
    B. Limiting fluid intake
    C. Keeping the head elevated
    D. Deep breathing

14. In chronic occlusive arterial disease, which of the following is MOST likely to be the cause of ulceration and gangrenous lesions?

    A. Trauma
    B. Emotional stress
    C. Stimulants such as caffeine
    D. Limited protein intake

15. Which of the following types of brain tumors occur MOST frequently?   15.____

    A. Glioma   B. Meningioma
    C. Neurofibroma   D. Pituitary adenoma

16. A 68-year-old client is admitted to the hospital with congestive heart failure and pulmo-   16.____
nary edema. Her treatment includes digoxin, Lasix, oxygen by mask, and a low-sodium
diet. She is restless and dyspneic.
For the client's comfort, the oxygen should be set at _____ L.

    A. 1-3   B. 2-5   C. 5-7   D. 12-15

17. It is possible to follow the course of prostate cancer by nonitoring the serum level of   17.____

    A. BUN (blood urea nitrogen)
    B. acid phosphatase
    C. albumin
    D. creatinine

18. Which of the following is a contraindication for an oxytocin challenge test (OCT)?   18.____

    A. Uterine activity   B. Hypertension
    C. Prematurity   D. Drug addiction

19. Which of the following is a guideline involved in suctioning a client with a tracheostomy?   19.____

    A. Using a new sterile catheter with each insertion
    B. Removing the inner cannula before inserting the suction catheter
    C. Initiating suction as catheter is being withdrawn
    D. Inserting the catheter until stimulating the cough reflex

20. A client experiences hemostasis due to prolonged bed rest after surgery. Other than   20.____
thrombus formation, which of the following pathological conditions is MOST likely to
result from this hemostasis?

    A. Gangrene of a limb   B. Cerebral aneurysm
    C. Coronary occlusion   D. Pulmonary embolism

21. If a client undergoes a parotidectomy to remove a cancerous lesion, which of the follow-   21.____
ing postoperative complications may cause distress for the client?

    A. Chvostek's sign
    B. A tracheostomy
    C. Increased salivation
    D. Dysfunctional facial nerve

22. Which of the following BEST describes the normal amniotic fluid of a pregnant client?   22.____

    A. Clear, almost colorless, with small white specks
    B. Milky, greenish-yellow, with small white specks
    C. Clear, with a tint of dark amber
    D. Cloudy, greenish-yellow, with shreds of mucus

23. A client is admitted to the hospital with a diagnosis of acute pulmonary edema. She appears extremely anxious. Which of the following medications would MOST likely be used to reduce her anxiety?

    A. Sodium phenobarbital   B. Morphine sulfate
    C. Chloral hydrate   D. Atarax

23._____

24. After undergoing a submucosal resection, a client should be observed for

    A. vomiting or spitting up blood
    B. temporal headache
    C. tremors
    D. periorbital crepitus

24._____

25. In which of the following fetal blood vessels is oxygen content typically HIGHEST?

    A. Ductus venosus   B. Ductus arteriosus
    C. Umbilical artery   D. Pulmonary artery

25._____

KEY (CORRECT ANSWERS)

1.	A		11.	D
2.	C		12.	C
3.	D		13.	A
4.	B		14.	A
5.	B		15.	A
6.	A		16.	C
7.	B		17.	B
8.	C		18.	C
9.	B		19.	C
10.	B		20.	D

21.	D
22.	A
23.	B
24.	A
25.	A

TEST 4

DIRECTIONS: Each question or incomplete statement is followed by several suggested answers or completions. Select the one that BEST answers the question or completes the statement. *PRINT THE LETTER OF THE CORRECT ANSWER IN THE SPACE AT THE RIGHT.*

1. A client is admitted with an acute episode of right side heart failure, and is receiving Lasix. During the admission history, the nurse should expect the client to complain of each of the following EXCEPT

    A. edema   B. nausea   C. fatigue   D. weakness

1.____

2. Which of the following drugs is contraindicated for clients who are receiving anticoagulants?

    A. Chloral hydrate   B. Thorazine
    C. Aspirin   D. Vasodilan

2.____

3. For Apgar scoring, the primary critical observation is

    A. the Moro reflex   B. heart rate
    C. presence of albumin   D. respiratory rate

3.____

4. Which of the following procedures would definitively differentiate between a gastric ulcer and gastric carcinoma?

    A. GI series   B. Gastroscopy
    C. Stool examination   D. Gastric analysis

4.____

5. Which of the following is suggested by laboratory results which show a bilirubin level above 2 mg/100 ml of blood volume?

    A. Pernicious anemia
    B. Decreased rate of red blood cell destruction
    C. Hemolytic anemia
    D. Increased cardiac output

5.____

6. Which of the following is a sign in muscle tissue of oxygen debt?

    A. Low lactic acid   B. High glycogen
    C. Low ATP   D. High calcium

6.____

7. Which of the following is included in the care of a client with placenta previa?

    A. Observing and recording the bleeding
    B. Vital signs at least twice per shift
    C. A high colonic enema after delivery
    D. Limiting ambulation until bleeding stops

7.____

8. Which of the following procedures is involved in preparing a client for a sigmoidoscopy?

    A. Collecting a stool specimen
    B. Administering an enema the morning of the examination
    C. Explaining to the client that a chalky substance will have to be swallowed
    D. Withholding all fluids within 24 hours prior to the examination

8.____

9. Cardiac nitrates are administered to a client in order to   9._____

    A.   improve cardiac output
    B.   relieve anginal pain
    C.   dilate superficial blood vessels
    D.   decrease blood pressure

10. To obtain maximum benefits after postural drainage, a patient should be encouraged to   10._____

    A.   remain in a sitting position
    B.   keep the legs elevated
    C.   cough deeply
    D.   rest for at least 30 minutes

11. A 23-year-old primigravida has missed two menstrual periods. The patient works a desk job in a large office. Which of the following recommendations would MOST likely be made by a nurse caring for this client?   11._____

    A.   Taking morning and afternoon breaks for extra nourishment
    B.   Attempting to get up and walk every few hours of the work day
    C.   Informing her employer that she cannot work past the second trimester
    D.   Taking morning and afternoon breaks to stretch her legs

12. The MOST likely cause of a spontaneous pneumothorax is   12._____

    A.   chest wall puncture   B.   subpleural bleb rupture
    C.   pleural friction rub   D.   tracheoesophageal fistula

13. When advising a patient about orthostatic hypotension, a nurse should inform the client that it can be adjusted by   13._____

    A.   wearing support hose
    B.   sitting on the edge of the bed for a short time before rising
    C.   lying down for thirty minutes after taking medication
    D.   avoiding high-energy tasks

14. Which of the following radioisotopes would MOST likely be used in brachytherapy of interstitial prostate cancer?   14._____

    A.   Gold-198   B.   Strontium-90
    C.   Iodine-131   D.   Phosphorus-32

15. Blood clotting requires the presence of which ion?   15._____

    A. Cl^- B. F^- C. Fe^{+++} D. Ca^{++}

16. Rotating tourniquets are used on a client suffering from acute pulmonary edema in order to   16._____

    A.   restrict visceral flow in the internal body cavities
    B.   decrease the flow of venous blood to the heart
    C.   increase the flow of blood through the capillaries
    D.   decrease the flow of arterial blood to the body

17. After a client has undergone a mastectomy, the client's arm on the affected side should   17.____
be positioned

   A. with the hand higher than the arm
   B. lower than the level of the right atrium
   C. in abduction, supported by pillows
   D. in adduction, surrounded by pillows

18. Which of the following BEST describes the normal respirations of a neonate?   18.____

   A. Regular, abdominal, 40-50 per minute, deep
   B. Irregular, thoracic, 30-60 per minute, deep
   C. Irregular, abdominal, 40-50 per minute, shallow
   D. Regular, thoracic, 40-60 per minute, shallow

19. Which of the following tests is MOST valuable in assisting a physician in prescribing an   19.____
effective antibiotic?

   A. Organ sensitivity   B. Susceptibility
   C. Serologic   D. Tissue culture

20. A 50-year-old patient is admitted to the hospital complaining of chest pain and shortness   20.____
of breath. The diagnosis of myocardial infarction is made.
Each of the following laboratory tests will likely be conducted to confirm this diagnosis
EXCEPT

   A. LDH   B. AST   C. SGPT   D. CK-MB

21. Which of the following is a contraindication for breastfeeding?   21.____

   A. Inverted nipples   B. Herpes genitalis
   C. Pregnancy   D. Mastitis

22. Which of the following is the primary nursing care objective for a client with acute lym-   22.____
phocytic leukemia who is undergoing a chemotherapeutic protocol?

   A. Checking vital signs every 4 hours
   B. Avoiding contact with infected persons
   C. Preventing all physical activity
   D. Increasing fluid intake

23. Cervical polyps   23.____

   A. will only cause bleeding if they are malignant
   B. are usually benign, but curettage is always performed to rule out malignancy
   C. frequently signal the onset of cervical cancer
   D. are usually malignant, and curettage is always performed

24. Which of the following blood proteins is involved in impairment of a client's immune sys-   24.____
tem?

   A. Globulin   B. Hemoglobin
   C. Thrombin   D. Albumin

25. An infant delivered at 29 weeks gestation, weighing 3 pounds, 7 ounces, would be classi-   25.____
    fied as

    A. nonviable   B. immature
    C. low birthweight   D. preterm

KEY (CORRECT ANSWERS)

1.	B	11.	B
2.	C	12.	B
3.	B	13.	B
4.	B	14.	A
5.	C	15.	D
6.	C	16.	B
7.	A	17.	A
8.	B	18.	C
9.	B	19.	A
10.	C	20.	C

21.	C
22.	B
23.	B
24.	A
25.	D

EXAMINATION SECTION
TEST 1

DIRECTIONS: Each question or incomplete statement is followed by several suggested answers or completions. Select the one that BEST answers the question or completes the statement. *PRINT THE LETTER OF THE CORRECT ANSWER IN THE SPACE AT THE RIGHT.*

Questions 1-2.

DIRECTIONS: Questions 1 through 2 are to be answered on the basis of the following information.

A newborn child has microsomia, flat nose, protruding tongue, low set ears, brushfield spots on the iris, muscle hypotonia, and cardiac Cushing defects. He is diagnosed with Down's syndrome.

1. Nursing interventions to keep this child free from infection include all of the following EXCEPT   1._____

    A.   preventing exposure to individuals with upper respiratory infections
    B.   encouraging optimal nutrition and adequate rest
    C.   keeping immunizations up to date
    D.   preventing exposure to individuals with AIDS

2. All of the following nursing procedures regarding nutrition for this child are correct EXCEPT   2._____

    A.   use of a bulb syringe to clear nasal passages before feeding
    B.   providing low roughage and minimal fluids
    C.   adjusting caloric requirement based on child's size
    D.   using a long-handled infant spoon to place food to side and back of mouth

3. A patient with spina bifida is admitted to the hospital. Nursing interventions to prevent post-operative complications include   3._____

    A.   position on side or prone
    B.   protect sac with sponge doughnut when holding infant
    C.   observe leakage of CSF from sac
    D.   all of the above

4. Nursing interventions that will maintain the child's skin integrity include all of the following EXCEPT   4._____

    A.   observing for redness and breaks in the skin
    B.   massaging pressure areas to promote circulation
    C.   avoiding frequent position changes
    D.   using a sheepskin or water mattress

5. Nursing interventions that will ensure minimal lower extremity deformity include all of the following EXCEPT   5._____

A.   providing passive ROM exercises
B.   keeping hips adducted using blanket rolls
C.   reassuring the parents and asking them to help the child in coping with the problem
D.   providing physical therapy

Questions 6-9.

DIRECTIONS: Questions 6 through 9 are to be answered on the basis of the following infor-
              mation.

A four-week-old male has had projectile vomiting for the last two days. Since yesterday
he has been constipated. Upon examination, a firm mobile mass is present in the right upper
region.

6.   This history typically favors the diagnosis of   6._____

     A.   tracheoesophageal fistula
     B.   gastritis
     C.   pyloric stenosis
     D.   cystic fibrosis

7.   Pre-operative nursing preparation of this patient includes all of the following EXCEPT   7._____

     A.   frequently assessing vital signs and signs of dehydration
     B.   withholding pacifier while NPO
     C.   carefully monitoring input/output and urine specific gravity
     D.   maintaining nasogastric decompression as ordered

8.   Post-operative nursing care of this child to keep him free from vomiting and maintaining   8._____
     good nutrition includes all of the following EXCEPT

     A.   initiating glucose water or electrolytes solution 4-6 hours post-operatively and
          gradually shifting to full strength formula
     B.   positioning the patient on his right side in a semi-Fowler's position after feeding
     C.   giving large infrequent feedings
     D.   teaching his parents how to feed him

9.   Nursing interventions to keep the patient free from infection include   9._____

     A.   observing operative site routinely for any drainage or signs of inflammation
     B.   performing incision care and dressing changes as ordered
     C.   assessing for signs of peritonitis
     D.   all of the above

10. A boy is admitted to the hospital for surgery for a cleft lip and palate.   10._____
     Pre-operative nursing interventions to maintain adequate nutrition and prevent aspira-
     tion include all of the following EXCEPT

     A.   feeding infant slowly in upright position
     B.   using a hard nipple and placing it inside the cleft
     C.   rinsing mouth with water after feeding to keep lip and palate clean
     D.   teaching parents how to feed and burp the child

11. Post-operative nursing interventions to keep the above patient free from infection and trauma do NOT include

    A. minimizing crying by holding and soothing infant as needed
    B. allowing pacifier use for a maximum of 1 hour per day
    C. maintaining logan bar on upper lip to decrease tension on suture line
    D. cleansing suture line after feeding with sterile swabs and solution as ordered to limit crusting and inflammation

11.____

Questions 12-13.

DIRECTIONS: Questions 12 and 13 are to be answered on the basis of the following information.

    A child is admitted to the hospital with a history of recurrent pneumonia and intestinal obstruction. After thorough examination, a diagnosis of cystic fibrosis is made.

12. Nursing interventions to maintain effective airway clearance and prevention of respiratory complications include all of the following EXCEPT

    A. teaching parents the use of nebulizer and carrying out of postural drainage and percussion
    B. teaching child breathing exercises and encouraging physical activities
    C. encouraging treatments immediately after meals
    D. observing and recording sputum amount, color, and consistency

12.____

13. Nursing discharge plans to make the parents and child learn to cope with the chronic nature of this disease include

    A. discouraging parents from over-protecting child
    B. encouraging child to assume age-appropriate responsibility for care to increase feelings of control
    C. plan exercise program that allows for optimal growth and development
    D. all of the above

13.____

14. Nursing interventions to maintain the integrity of a surgical repair of hypospadias in a 7 year-old child do NOT include

    A. checking pressure dressing for evidence of bleeding and to ensure intact dressing
    B. washing the repaired area daily
    C. monitoring the function of urinary diversion apparatus
    D. checking for adequate circulation to the tip of the penis

14.____

15. A 1-year-old girl has prolonged neonatal jaundice. A physical examination shows coarse facies with large open fontanelles, protruding tongue, umbilical hernia, and hypotonia. A diagnosis of congenital hypothyroidism is made.
Nursing interventions to maintain the growth and development of the patient include

    A. dispelling any fears about abnormal growth and development
    B. teaching the parents about medication administration, side effects, and the need for lifelong administration
    C. monitoring child's growth and development monthly
    D. all of the above

15.____

Questions 16-20.

DIRECTIONS: Questions 16 through 20 are to be answered on the basis of the following information.

A 29-year-old white male of average height and build presents with polyuria and polydip-
sia. A laboratory examination reveals a blood glucose of 295 mg/dl.

16. Nursing education of this patient in regard to insulin injection includes all of the following   16._____
EXCEPT:

    A.   Insulin must be well below room temperature before use
    B.   Rotating injection sites so that no individual site is used more frequently than once
       a month
    C.   Injecting at a 45° or 90° angle, depending on subcutaneous tissue layer thickness
    D.   Avoiding smoking for 30 minutes after injection

17. Nursing instructions to the patient regarding monitoring of blood glucose do NOT include   17._____

    A.   the principles of urine testing
    B.   common medications that interfere with urine test results, e.g., aspirin, vitamin C,
       and cephalosporin, etc.
    C.   the formula for determining insulin dosage
    D.   the need for accurate date and time records for both urine and fingerstick testing

18. Nursing instructions to aid the patient in establishing and maintaining a pattern of regular   18._____
exercise include all of the following EXCEPT

    A.   performing exercise after meals to ensure an adequate level of blood glucose
    B.   excessive or unplanned exercise may trigger hyper-glycemia
    C.   taking insulin before active exercise but avoid injection into an exercising limb
    D.   carrying a rapid-acting source of glucose

19. Diabetic foot care does NOT include   19._____

    A.   wearing properly fitted shoes
    B.   using lanolin cream or oil to prevent dryness and cracking of feet
    C.   visiting a podiatrist as needed for care of nails, calluses, and corns
    D.   using a fungicidal agent to prevent athlete's foot

20. Nursing interventions to teach the patient how to avoid problems associated with ketoac-   20._____
idosis include

    A.   correcting dehydration by administration of IV fluids
    B.   correcting blood glucose by administration of regular insulin
    C.   wearing a diabetic alert bracelet or tag at all times
    D.   all of the above

KEY (CORRECT ANSWERS)

1.	B	6.	C	11.	B	16.	A
2.	B	7.	B	12.	C	17.	C
3.	D	8.	C	13.	D	18.	B
4.	C	9.	D	14.	B	19.	D
5.	B	10.	B	15.	B	20.	D

TEST 2

DIRECTIONS: Each question or incomplete statement is followed by several suggested answers or completions. Select the one that BEST answers the question or completes the statement. *PRINT THE LETTER OF THE CORRECT ANSWER IN THE SPACE AT THE RIGHT.*

1. A 45-year-old white female has acute abdominal pain, nausea and vomiting, dyspepsia, and acute tenderness in the right upper quadrant.
   Nursing interventions for this patient do NOT include relieving

   A. pain with morphine
   B. reflex spasms with antispasmodic drugs PRN as ordered
   C. vomiting and decreasing gastric stimulation with nasogastric tube to suction
   D. all of the above

   1.____

2. Post-operative nursing care for a patient with a T tube includes all of the following EXCEPT

   A. avoiding tension and obstruction of the tubing
   B. removing the T tube 24-48 hours after the operation
   C. measuring the amount of drainage carefully
   D. 3-4 days after the operation, clamping as ordered before meals to allow bile to drain into the duodenum

   2.____

Questions 3-6.

DIRECTIONS: Questions 3 through 6 are to be answered on the basis of the following information.

A 65-year-old alcoholic male is admitted to the floor with abdominal distention, jaundice, and slight impairment of consciousness. After a thorough examination, alcoholic cirrhosis is diagnosed.

3. Nursing interventions in the prevention of bleeding problems do NOT include

   A. avoiding injections and applying pressure to veni-puncture sites for at least 5 minutes
   B. monitoring prothrombin time, platelet count, white blood cells, and PTT
   C. handling patient gently and preventing scratching from pruritis
   D. restraining patient with padded restraints

   3.____

4. Nursing interventions to reduce ascites and promote comfort include all of the following EXCEPT

   A. bed rest or restricted activity
   B. high protein/high sodium diet
   C. measuring abdominal girth at umbilicus at least once every shift
   D. administering diuretics as ordered

   4.____

5. If paracentesis is to be performed, nursing care of the patient includes   5.____

    A. sedating the patient before the procedure
    B. not allowing patient to void before the procedure
    C. preparing the patient for a sitting or high Fowler's position during the procedure
    D. maintaining patency of the puncture site

6. Nursing intervention to assist the surgeon with insertion of a Sengstaken-Blakemore tube includes   6.____

    A. ensuring balloon patency and accurate labeling of all parts before insertion
    B. monitoring balloon pressure frequently
    C. helping patient expectorate secretions or gently suctioning secretions from oral cavity
    D. all of the above

Questions 7-8.

DIRECTIONS: Questions 7 and 8 are to be answered on the basis of the following information.

A 45-year-old female with previous H/O gallbladder disease presents with pain in left upper quadrant, vomiting, and abdominal distention. She is a moderate alcohol user. After a thorough examination, acute pancreatitis is diagnosed.

7. Nursing interventions to keep this patient free of pain include all of the following EXCEPT   7.____

    A. administration of morphine
    B. keep NPO until inflammation subsides and serum amylase levels fall
    C. suctioning nasogastric tube if vomiting is severe or ileus is present
    D. administering antacids frequently in mild casesgt

8. Nursing interventions to maintain adequate nutrition do NOT include   8.____

    A. administering total parenteral nutrition as ordered if inflammation present
    B. gradually progressing to a high fat diet after inflammation subsides
    C. teaching avoidance of stimulants and alcohol
    D. all of the above

Questions 9-10.

DIRECTIONS: Questions 9 and 10 are to be answered on the basis of the following information.

An 18-year-old has pain and tenderness in the right upper quadrant of his abdomen, mild fever, malaise, and vomiting. Examination reveals his liver is enlarged and hepatitis is diagnosed.

9. Nursing interventions to maintain adequate nutrition in this patient include all of the following EXCEPT   9.____

    A. a well-balanced diet with adequate nutrients and calories
    B. administering mild antiemetics as needed before meals

C. a high fat diet with minimal fluid intake
D. having food available at patient's bedside

10. The nurse should provide health education about preventive measures by   10._____

    A. advising against washing clothing in hot water
    B. encouraging optimal sensation and hygiene
    C. advising regular blood donations
    D. all of the above

Questions 11-12.

DIRECTIONS: Questions 11 and 12 are to be answered on the basis of the following information.

A 35-year-old female comes to the infertility clinic for an evaluation. She states that she has had some weight gain, constipation, and is easily fatigued. Upon examination, she has dry skin, coarse thin hairs, and a thick tongue. Hypothyroidism is diagnosed by the examining physician.

11. All of the following complications may be expected in this patient EXCEPT   11._____

    A. myxedema   B. thyroid strom
    C. organic psychosis   D. cretinism

12. Nursing interventions to return the patient to the euthyroid state include all of the following EXCEPT   12._____

    A. increasing physical activity and sensory stimulation gradually as condition improves
    B. providing a cold environment conducive to rest
    C. assisting patient in choosing a low-calorie diet
    D. avoiding use of all sedatives

Questions 13-14.

DIRECTIONS: Questions 13 and 14 are to be answered on the basis of the following information.

A 40-year-old male is admitted with muscle weakness, fatigue, abdominal pain, anorexia, nausea, and increased pigmentation of the skin and mucous membranes. Laboratory tests show low serum sodium and glucose, elevated serum potassium, and low serum cortisol levels.

13. All of the following are signs or symptoms of adrenal crises EXCEPT   13._____

    A. severe headache or abdominal pain
    B. confusion, restlessness, or coma
    C. hypertension
    D. nausea and diarrhea

14. Nursing interventions to maintain a normal hormonal balance do NOT include   14.____

    A. maintaining a regular activity pattern by balancing activity and rest
    B. promoting good nutrition, monitoring weight, fluid status and input/output
    C. eliminating all sources of stress
    D. all of the above

Questions 15-16.

DIRECTIONS: Questions 15 and 16 are to be answered on the basis of the following information.

A 42-year-old female with Cushing's syndrome is admitted to the hospital.

15. Nursing interventions to help the patient manage the symptoms effectively include all of   15.____
the following EXCEPT

    A. protecting the patient from unnecessary exposure to infection
    B. providing an atmosphere conducive to rest and spacing activities over time
    C. providing a diet high in calories and sodium and low in potassium
    D. assessing mental status regularly

16. Nursing interventions to keep this patient free from complications after adrenalectomy   16.____
include

    A. measuring urine output accurately and frequently
    B. minimizing physiological and psychological stress
    C. monitoring wound healing carefully
    D. all of the above

Questions 17-18.

DIRECTIONS: Questions 17 and 18 are to be answered on the basis of the following information.

A 39-year-old male hyperthyroid patient is discharged from the hospital after treatment
with radioactive iodine.

17. Nursing advice to the patient should include all of the following EXCEPT   17.____

    A. avoiding close contact with children or pregnant women for 24 hours
    B. decreasing fluid intake and avoid emptying bladder
    C. flushing toilet 2-3 times after each use
    D. recognizing symptoms of hypothyroidism and maintaining follow-up program

18. Nursing care of a patient with transphenoidal hypophysectomy includes   18.____

    A. frequent gentle oral care and assessment for patency of gingival suture line
    B. monitoring for CSF leak through muscle plug in nose
    C. teaching patient about the need for lifelong hormone replacement therapy and regular medical follow-up
    D. all of the above

Questions 19-20.

DIRECTIONS: Questions 19 and 20 are to be answered on the basis of the following informa-
               tion.

A 35-year-old male with renal colic is admitted to the hospital. He is in a state of extreme
anxiety and apprehension. Any voluntary movement results in tremors of the hands.

19.   All of the following are possible causes of hypoparathy-roidism in this patient EXCEPT   19._____

      A.   accidental removal during thyroidectomy
      B.   auto-immune or familial hypoparathyroidism
      C.   accidental ingestion of synthroid
      D.   resistance to parathyroid action

20.   Nursing interventions in the management of this case do NOT include   20._____

      A.   instructing patient about signs and symptoms of hypocalcemia that should be
           reported
      B.   administering thyroid extract and warning of probable constipation
      C.   checking for positive Trousseau's or Chvostek's sign
      D.   assessing neuro-muscular status frequently

Questions 21-25.

DIRECTIONS: Questions 21 through 25 are to be answered on the basis of the following infor-
               mation.

A 29-year-old male is admitted with the diagnosis of severe depression

21.   Nursing interventions to keep the patient protected from suicidal gestures include all of   21._____
      the following EXCEPT

      A.   assuming responsibilities for safety of patient by restricting him to observable
           areas
      B.   avoiding all discussion of suicide
      C.   allowing patient to express his feelings
      D.   providing realistic reassurance, conveying attitude that patient will succeed

22.   The patient is scheduled for ECT.   22._____
      Nursing interventions to keep the patient free from injury include all of the following
      EXCEPT

      A.   explaining the procedure thoroughly and answering patient's questions and con-
           cerns
      B.   giving medications as ordered, e.g., muscle relaxant atropine sulphate and short-
           acting barbiturate for sedation
      C.   placing patient in bed restraints upon return from procedure
      D.   monitoring vital signs every 15 minutes for the first hour and hourly for the next 4
           hours

23. Nursing interventions that will increase patient interactions with the staff, other patients, and his family include

    23.____

    A. helping patient to identify, define, and solve difficult problems in social relationships
    B. practicing social skills and use of role playing
    C. involving patient in activities that provide the chance for success
    D. all of the above

24. The nurse should help family members maintain their relationship with the patient by

    24.____

    A. providing them with an opportunity to confront the patient with their feelings of anger, guilt, and inability to help him
    B. helping the family to understand patient's anger, dependency, and negativism
    C. developing a set of expectations for the patient and a schedule for meeting these expectations
    D. all of the above

25. Nursing guidelines for dealing with a patient with overanxious behavior includes all of the following EXCEPT

    25.____

    A. helping patient express feelings about stressful situations and unmet needs
    B. being judgmental and offering only conditional acceptance
    C. offering reassurance by giving appropriate information and correcting misinformation
    D. helping patient identify situations that trigger anxiety

---

KEY (CORRECT ANSWERS)

1.	A		11.	B
2.	B		12.	B
3.	D		13.	C
4.	B		14.	C
5.	C		15.	C
6.	D		16.	D
7.	A		17.	B
8.	B		18.	D
9.	C		19.	C
10.	B		20.	B

21.	B
22.	C
23.	D
24.	B
25.	B

EXAMINATION SECTION
TEST 1

DIRECTIONS: Each question or incomplete statement is followed by several suggested answers or completions. Select the one that BEST answers the question or completes the statement. *PRINT THE LETTER OF THE CORRECT ANSWER IN THE SPACE AT THE RIGHT.*

1. According to Freudian theory, the _____ functions to encourage a person's tolerance of frustration.

    A. subconscious   B. id
    C. ego   D. superego

1.____

2. Which of the following hormones controls the use of glucose by the body's cells?

    A. Cortisone   B. Insulin
    C. Adrenal steroids   D. Thyroxine

2.____

3. A client who is receiving lithium carbonate should undergo regular monitoring of

    A. blood pressure   B. blood level
    C. weight   D. urine

3.____

4. According to intrapsychic theory, the problem of separation anxiety is MOST likely to occur during the _____ stage.

    A. latency   B. oral   C. anal   D. phallic

4.____

5. A client with adrenal insufficiency is weak and dizzy upon arising in the morning. The MOST likely cause of this is

    A. lack of sodium
    B. increased intracavity fluid volume
    C. hypertension
    D. hypoglycemic reaction

5.____

6. The administration of Anectine prior to electroconvulsive therapy involves the major complication of

    A. loss of bowel control
    B. inhibition of breathing muscles
    C. memory loss
    D. the bite reflex

6.____

7. An infant with congenital hyperthyroidism is at risk for _____ if care is not given immediately.

    A. thyrotoxicosis   B. acromegaly
    C. myxedema   D. mental retardation

7.____

8. For which of the following is lithium carbonate used as a control or modifier?

    A. Manic episode of bipolar disorder
    B. Acute agitation of schizophrenia

8.____

C. Agitated phase of paranoia
D. Depressive phase of major depression

9. Which of the following is the cause of acromegaly?   9.____

A. Oversecretion of adrenal steroids
B. Undersecretion of thyroid hormone
C. Oversecretion of growth hormone
D. Undersecretion of testosterone

10. At what approximate age does a person demonstrate the primary emergence of his or   10.____
her personality?

A. 6 months   B. 18 months
C. 2 years   D. 8 years

11. Diabetic acidosis is caused by elevated _____ levels in the blood.   11.____

A. lactic acid   B. ketone
C. albumin   D. glucose

12. Which of the following behaviors is MOST likely to be demonstrated by an autistic child?   12.____

A. Lack of response to external stimuli
B. Sad facial expression
C. Irrelevant smiling
D. Rocking and flapping of hands

13. To evaluate the effectiveness of DDAVP in treating diabetes insipidus, which of the fol-   13.____
lowing should be monitored?

A. Blood pressure   B. Intake and output
C. Pulse rate   D. Serum glucose

14. Glucagon   14.____

A. retards glycogenesis
B. causes the release of insulin
C. elevates blood sugar levels
D. improves the storage of glucose

15. Of the following, the clearest evidence of mental illness is when a client   15.____

A. does not seem to be able to complete tasks
B. has difficulty relating to others
C. has little interest in social activities or work
D. encounters frequent periods of high anxiety

16. For a client with insulin-dependent diabetes mellitus, insulin needs will *decrease* when   16.____
the client

A. exercises   B. is infected
C. reaches middle age   D. is emotionally stressed

17. The treatment for a client suffering from depression should focus on getting the client to 17.____
    A. express anger toward others
    B. admit an emotional problem
    C. articulate feelings of low self-esteem
    D. accept care and comfort willingly

18. A child who is about to undergo surgery to correct a congenital megacolon should be given a preoperative enema of 18.____
    A. barium
    B. isotonic saline
    C. tap water
    D. hypertonic phosphate

19. Which of the following is a common side effect associated with the use of Thorazine? 19.____
    A. Jaundice
    B. Melanocytosis
    C. Photosensitivity
    D. Excessive thirst

20. Piaget's theory of cognitive development states that at the age of six months, an infant should demonstrate 20.____
    A. a sense of time
    B. the ability to remember
    C. the onset of object permanence
    D. coordinated motor responses

21. Which of the following would MOST clearly reveal congenital hip dysplasia in a newborn infant? 21.____
    A. Different leg lengths
    B. Asymmetrical gluteal folds
    C. Limited adduction
    D. Skewed leg alignment

22. A client is diagnosed with an organic mental disorder. Which of the following nursing strategies would be MOST helpful to this client? 22.____
    A. Providing a diet high in carbohydrates
    B. Providing a variety of stimuli to keep the client's interest high
    C. Eliminating the need for choices
    D. Asking the client for input concerning the nursing care plan

23. Which of the following would be included in the early treatment of diabetic acidosis? 23.____
    A. IV fluids
    B. Kayexalate
    C. Potassium
    D. NPH insulin

24. Which level of consciousness BEST represents a person's feelings and attitudes? 24.____
    A. Conscious
    B. Unconscious
    C. Preconscious
    D. Foreconscious

25. What is the MOST common cause of diabetic ketoacidosis?   25.____

    A. Inadequate fluid intake   B. Psychological stress
    C. Elevated insulin level   D. Infection

KEY (CORRECT ANSWERS)

1.	C		11.	B
2.	C		12.	D
3.	B		13.	B
4.	B		14.	C
5.	D		15.	B
6.	B		16.	A
7.	D		17.	A
8.	A		18.	B
9.	C		19.	C
10.	C		20.	C

21.	B
22.	C
23.	A
24.	B
25.	D

TEST 2

DIRECTIONS: Each question or incomplete statement is followed by several suggested answers or completions. Select the one that BEST answers the question or completes the statement. *PRINT THE LETTER OF THE CORRECT ANSWER IN THE SPACE AT THE RIGHT.*

1. A client with an anxiety disorder is likely to handle the anxiety in each of the following ways EXCEPT   1.____

   A. projecting it onto nonthreatening objects
   B. converting it into a physical symptom
   C. demonstrating regressive behavior
   D. acting out with antisocial behavior

2. What type of diet is recommended for a client with Graves' disease?   2.____

   A. High roughage   B. Low sodium
   C. Liquid   D. High-calorie

3. Which of the following is the cause of primary degenerative dementia?   3.____

   A. Anatomic brain changes
   B. Atrophy of the frontal lobes
   C. An extended history of malnutrition
   D. Excessive use of narcotics

4. Which of the following blood gas results would indicate diabetic acidosis?   4.____

   A. Reduced HCO_3 B. Elevated pH
   C. Reduced PO_2 D. Elevated PCO_2

5. The primary difference between a psychophysiologic disorder and a somatoform disorder is that a   5.____

   A. psychophysiologic disorder involves an actual change in tissues
   B. somatoform disorder is caused by emotions
   C. psychophysiologic disorder restricts the client's activities
   D. somatoform disorder is accompanied by a feeling of illness

6. Which of the following is MOST likely to be a complication following the insertion of a ventriculoperitoneal shunt
   in a child with communicating hydrocephalus?   6.____

   A. Violent tremors
   B. Distended abdomen
   C. Yellowish discharge from shunt
   D. Fever

7. Each of the following is a common physiological response to anxiety EXCEPT   7.____

   A. respiratory constriction
   B. dilated pupils
   C. hyperglycemia
   D. increased pulse rate

8. It is MOST important for a nurse to monitor a client suffering from alcohol and cirrhosis for   8.____

    A. gastric pain   B. blood in the stool
    C. dizziness   D. constipation

9. To encourage a withdrawn and noncommunicative client to talk, the BEST nursing plan would include the attempt to   9.____

    A. ask the client to describe feelings
    B. ask simply-phrased questions that require yes or no answers
    C. join the client in an activity that the client enjoys
    D. concentrate on subjects that are nonthreatening

10. What is the function of glucose in a cell?   10.____

    A. Energy extraction   B. Protein synthesis
    C. Cellular respiration   D. Genetic coding

11. Which of the following treatments would be included in a plan for a client with severe and intractable depression and suicidal tendency?   11.____

    A. High doses of tranquilizers
    B. Electroconvulsive therapy
    C. Nondirective psychotherapy
    D. Thorazine

12. A *decrease* in the anterior pituitary secretion of ACTH would be caused by   12.____

    A. ketosis
    B. a *decrease* in the blood concentration of adrenal steroids
    C. an *increase* in the blood concentration of cortisol
    D. acidosis

13. A client is experiencing a phase of extreme elation and hyperactivity. Which of the following nursing interventions would BEST meet the client's nutritional needs?   13.____

    A. Assuming that the client will eat when hungry
    B. Firmly suggesting that the client sit and eat the meal that has been prepared
    C. Inducing an IV feeding to insure that the client is properly nourished
    D. Giving the client frequent high-calorie feedings that the client can feed to herself

14. Which of the following would be experienced by a client with acute cholecystitis accompanied by biliary colic?   14.____

    A. Melena
    B. Lipid intolerance
    C. Diarrhea
    D. Pain in lower left quadrant

15. Which of the following must be monitored especially closely following a hypophysectomy?   15.____

    A. Motor reflexes   B. Urinary output
    C. Intracranial pressure   D. Respiration

16. Which of the following would MOST accurately characterize the personality of a client   16._____
with obsessive-compulsive personality disorder?

    A. Deep depression   B. Indecisiveness and doubt
    C. Rapid mood swings   D. Detailed delusions

17. Which of the following symptoms would MOST likely be revealed during an assessment   17._____
of a client with Cushing's syndrome?

    A. Dehydration   B. Migraine headaches
    C. Menorrhagia   D. Hypertension

18. Most commonly, the behavior of a client with schizophrenia can be described as   18._____

    A. euphoric   B. angry and hostile
    C. flat and apathetic   D. depressed

19. Which of the following medications would be used to treat a child with cystic fibrosis?   19._____

    A. Antimetabolite   B. Pancreatic enzymes
    C. Fat-soluble vitamins   D. Aerosol mists

20. Which of the following would NOT be a helpful component of a nursing care plan for a   20._____
severely depressed client?

    A. Short-term projects
    B. Client participation in activity planning
    C. Repetitive activities
    D. Simple instructions to be followed

21. A client with Addison's disease is experiencing hypotension. Most likely, this involves a   21._____
disturbance in the production of

    A. mineralocorticoids   B. proteins
    C. glucocorticoids   D. insulin

22. Which of the following medications would be used to counter an overdose of narcotics?   22._____

    A. Methadone   B. Thorazine
    C. Benzedrine   D. Narcan

23. Prior to a serum glucose test, a client with Type II diabetes mellitus should   23._____

    A. have a clear liquid breakfast
    B. take prescribed medications
    C. void the bladder
    D. avoid food and fluids

24. Which of the following is the BEST description of a somatoform disorder?   24._____
A(n)

    A. conscious defense against stress
    B. sublimation of stress
    C. psychological defense against anxiety
    D. unconscious means of controlling conflict

25. Which of the following tests is conducted to detect PKU in infant children?   25.____

    A. OCT   B. Phenistix test
    C. BUN   D. Guthrie blood test

KEY (CORRECT ANSWERS)

1.	D		11.	B
2.	D		12.	C
3.	B		13.	D
4.	A		14.	B
5.	A		15.	C
6.	D		16.	B
7.	A		17.	B
8.	B		18.	C
9.	D		19.	B
10.	A		20.	B

21.	A
22.	D
23.	D
24.	D
25.	D

TEST 3

DIRECTIONS: Each question or incomplete statement is followed by several suggested answers or completions. Select the one that BEST answers the question or completes the statement. *PRINT THE LETTER OF THE CORRECT ANSWER IN THE SPACE AT THE RIGHT.*

1. A client recently admitted to an alcohol detoxification unit would probably exhibit each of the following EXCEPT

    A. hypertension   B. nausea
    C. hyperactivity   D. loss of appetite

1.____

2. Prior to an adrenalectomy, the client should

    A. increase fluid intake
    B. receive steroids
    C. have all medication withheld for 48 hours
    D. be placed on a high-protein diet

2.____

3. A client with an antisocial personality disorder

    A. learns quickly through experience and punishment
    B. is generally unable to defer gratification
    C. often masks his disorder by articulate communication
    D. suffers from a high level of anxiety

3.____

4. Which of the following is a defense mechanism that helps an individual channel unacceptable desires into socially approved behavior?

    A. Regression   B. Denial
    C. Conversion   D. Sublimation

4.____

5. Which of the following would NOT be a likely result of a laboratory test performed on a client suffering from diabetic ketoacidosis?

    A. Low CO_2 B. Increased acidity
    C. High bicarbonate   D. Increased blood sugar

5.____

6. Following an adrenalectomy, a client is MOST likely to exhibit the symptoms of

    A. sodium retention   B. dehydration
    C. hypotension   D. increased urinary output

6.____

7. It is MOST important for a nurse to _____ when attempting to resolve a crisis situation with a client.

    A. encourage socialization
    B. meet all of the client's dependency needs
    C. nurture the client's ego strengths
    D. introduce the client to a therapy group

7.____

8. Which of the following is NOT a typical indication of a hypoglycemic reaction to insulin?

    A. Paleness   B. Excessive thirst
    C. Tremors   D. Perspiration

8.____

9. A client is admitted to the hospital with a diagnosis of conversion disorder. The nurse should expect the client's attitude toward his physical symptoms to be one of
    9.____

    A. hysteria
    B. indifference
    C. anger
    D. great sadness

10. Along with vitamin D, the regulatory agent that controls the overall calcium balance in the body is
    10.____

    A. parathyroid hormone
    B. growth hormone
    C. thyroid hormone
    D. ACTH

11. A client is admitted to the hospital with Wernicke's encephalopathy caused by chronic alcoholism. The client's initial treatment would include
    11.____

    A. an increase in fluid intake
    B. IM injection of thiamine
    C. administration of an anti-opiate
    D. administration of paraldehyde

12. Each of the following is a defect commonly associated with tetralogy of Fallot EXCEPT
    12.____

    A. pulmonary artery stenosis
    B. mitral valve stenosis
    C. right ventricular hypertrophy
    D. overriding aorta

13. Which of the following statements, spoken to a nurse by a patient diagnosed with Alzheimer's disease, would indicate a need to accomplish Erikson's developmental task of ego integrity versus despair?
    13.____

    A. I don't understand why I have to go through this.
    B. Please leave me alone.
    C. I can take care of myself.
    D. I am useless to everyone now.

14. The purpose of administering Mycifradin to a client with liver disease is to
    14.____

    A. increase the urea digestive activity of enteric bacteria
    B. protect the liver from bacteria
    C. reduce ammonia-forming bacteria in the intestinal tract
    D. aid the digestion of complex proteins

15. Emotionally disturbed children
    15.____

    A. seem unresponsive to their environment
    B. respond equally to all stimuli
    C. respond violently to most stimuli
    D. are immersed in their environment to the point of distraction

16. A client exhibiting cold intolerance may have
    16.____

    A. increased levels of CO_2
    B. decreased blood pH

C. insufficient bile salts
D. decreased levels of T_3 and T_4

17. The part of the psyche that develops from internalizing the concepts of parents and other significant relations is the 17.____

A. foreconscious
C. ego
B. id
D. superego

18. Which of the following is NOT a typical sign of hypo-kalemia? 18.____

A. Weakness
C. Edema
B. Abdominal distention
D. Apathy

19. Which of the following might be experienced by a person who makes an abrupt withdrawal from habitual use of barbiturates? 19.____

A. Gastric bleeding
C. Convulsions
B. Cardiac arrhythmia
D. Ataxia

20. Which of the following would be observed in a toddler with cyanotic congenital heart disease? 20.____

A. Orthopnea
C. Increased hematocrit
B. Blotchy skin
D. Pitting edema

21. A delusional client is admitted for psychiatric treatment after harming a close relative. In talking about the incident, the client refers to herself in the third person. This is an example of the defense mechanism of 21.____

A. conversion
C. dissociation
B. transference
D. displacement

22. Which of the following is the clearest indication of diabetes insipidus? 22.____

A. Elevated blood glucose
B. Increased blood pressure
C. Decreased urinary specific gravity
D. Increased BUN

23. Which of the following is the MOST common cause of functional mental illness? 23.____

A. Infection
C. Social environment
B. Chemical imbalance
D. Genes

24. Which gland regulates the rate of oxygenation in the body's cells? 24.____

A. Thyroid   B. Adrenal   C. Thalamus   D. Pituitary

25. Which of the following is NOT thought to be a significant formative component of personality? 25.____

A. Cultural setting
C. Psychologic development
B. Genetic background
D. Biologic constitution

KEY (CORRECT ANSWERS)

1.	C		11.	B
2.	B		12.	B
3.	B		13.	D
4.	D		14.	C
5.	C		15.	A
6.	C		16.	D
7.	C		17.	D
8.	B		18.	C
9.	B		19.	C
10.	A		20.	C

21.	C
22.	B
23.	C
24.	A
25.	B

TEST 4

DIRECTIONS: Each question or incomplete statement is followed by several suggested answers or completions. Select the one that BEST answers the question or completes the statement. *PRINT THE LETTER OF THE CORRECT ANSWER IN THE SPACE AT THE RIGHT.*

1. The preservation of sodium in the body's cells is accomplished by the hormone   1._____

    A. parathyroid hormone   B. thyrocalcitonin
    C. aldosterone   D. insulin

2. Which of the following behaviors would be LEAST likely to be demonstrated by a client   2._____
   with an organic mental disorder?

    A. An inclination to ignore the present circumstances while dwelling in the past
    B. A steadfast resistance to change
    C. The inability to focus on new interests
    D. A fixation on personal appearance and hygiene

3. Which of the following is a complication associated with hyperparathyroidism?   3._____

    A. Bone destruction   B. Graves' disease
    C. Hypotension   D. Tetany

4. Which of the following interventions should be undertaken to prevent thrombus formation   4._____
   in a client with sickle-cell anemia?

    A. Administer heparin or other anticoagulants
    B. Encourage exercise
    C. Maintain a high-roughage diet
    D. Increase oral fluid intake

5. A client with an obsessive-compulsive personality disorder will MOST likely react with   5._____
   _____ if he is interrupted in the performance of a ritual.

    A. hostility   B. indifference
    C. confusion   D. withdrawal

6. Which of the following would be experienced by a patient in a diabetic coma, but not by a   6._____
   patient in an HHNK coma?

    A. Kussmaul respirations   B. Glycosuria
    C. Fluid loss   D. Elevated blood glucose

7. Which of the following daily patterns tends to work best with clients who are depressed?   7._____

    A. Numerous sensory stimuli
    B. A simple daily schedule
    C. Removing the need for complicated decisions
    D. Multiple and varied activities

8. Glucocorticoids are secreted by the   8._____

    A. hypophysis cerebri   B. adrenal glands
    C. thyroid   D. pancreas

9. Prior to beginning lithium carbonate therapy, a client should undergo   9.____

    A. fluid and electrolyte evaluation
    B. renal evaluation
    C. psychomotor
    D. BUN evaluation

10. Which of the following is the result of an underproduction of thyroxin?   10.____

    A. Acromegaly   B. Cushing's disease
    C. Myxedema   D. Addison's disease

11. Which of the following is a common side effect of the major tranquilizers?   11.____

    A. Tremors   B. Diaphoresis
    C. Jaundice   D. Photosensitivity

12. Each of the following is likely to be revealed during the assessment of a client with hyper-   12.____
thyroidism EXCEPT

    A. weight loss   B. increased appetite
    C. constipation   D. nervousness

13. Severe emotional disturbances are often treated with tranquilizers to   13.____

    A. prevent complications
    B. make the client less dangerous to himself and others
    C. improve the client's mood
    D. make the client more receptive to psychotherapy

14. Which of the following symptoms would cause a nurse to stop giving Thorazine to a cli-   14.____
ent?

    A. Uncoordinated movements   B. Jaundice
    C. Withdrawal   D. Tremors

15. What is the MOST likely cause of ascites in a patient with cirrhosis?   15.____

    A. Inhibited portal venous return
    B. Undersecretion of bile salts
    C. Gastric bleeding
    D. Overproduction of serum albumin

16. The defense mechanism used by clients who express anxiety through physical symp-   16.____
toms can BEST be described as

    A. psychosomatic   B. regressive
    C. psychoneurotic   D. dissociative

17. A 42-year-old client is admitted to the hospital with a diagnosis of Addison's disease. She   17.____
is weak, hypotensive, and has low sodium and high potassium levels.
The focus of the client's therapy should be

    A. lowering the level of eosiniphils
    B. restoring electrolyte balance
    C. increasing carbohydrate intake
    D. increasing lymph

18. A client who has been hospitalized for major depression has recently begun to receive   18.____
    Parnate. It is important that the nurse explain to the client that the use of this drug

    A. typically causes extreme photosensitivity
    B. may cause drowsiness
    C. increases the heart rate
    D. involves dietary restrictions

19. The MOST frequent cause of Cushing's syndrome is   19.____

    A. hyperplasia of pituitary
    B. hyperplasia of adrenal cortex
    C. decreased adrenocortical hormones
    D. insufficient production of ACTH

20. A group setting is particularly conducive to therapy because it   20.____

    A. takes the focus off the individual client
    B. forces clients to notice similarities with others
    C. establishes a learning environment
    D. encourages individual relationships

21. What is the purpose of installing a T-tube after a cholecystectomy?   21.____

    A. Draining bile from the cystic duct
    B. Protecting the common bile duct
    C. Preventing infection
    D. Providing a port for cholangiogram dye

22. A nurse notices that a socially agressive elderly client, who has been receiving Thora-   22.____
    zine for several months, is sitting rigidly in a chair. What other adverse effects of the drug
    should the nurse watch for?

    A. Tremors   B. Slurred speech
    C. Excessive salivation   D. Withdrawal

23. For what reason is an infant born with a cleft palate prone to infection?   23.____

    A. Mouth breathing
    B. Leakage of nasal mucus
    C. Poor nutrition from feeding disturbances
    D. Poor circulation in defective locus

24. Which of the following is a defense mechanism in which emotional conflicts are   24.____
    expressed through sensorimotor or somatic disability?

    A. Dissociation   B. Conversion
    C. Displacement   D. Regression

25. For the emergency treatment of ketoacidosis, what type of insulin should be adminis-   25.____
    tered?

    A. Zinc suspension
    B. NPH insulin
    C. Protamine zinc suspension
    D. Regular insulin injection

KEY (CORRECT ANSWERS)

1.	C	11.	A
2.	D	12.	C
3.	A	13.	D
4.	D	14.	B
5.	A	15.	A
6.	A	16.	C
7.	B	17.	B
8.	D	18.	D
9.	B	19.	B
10.	C	20.	C

21.	B
22.	A
23.	A
24.	B
25.	D

EXAMINATION SECTION
TEST 1

DIRECTIONS: Each question or incomplete statement is followed by several suggested answers or completions. Select the one that BEST answers the question or completes the statement. *PRINT THE LETTER OF THE CORRECT ANSWER IN THE SPACE AT THE RIGHT.*

Questions 1-4.

DIRECTIONS: Questions 1 through 4 are to be answered on the basis of the following information.

A 45-year-old patient is admitted with a severe frontal headache. After a thorough examination, meningitis is ruled out. A CT scan of the head shows multiple ring enhancing lesions. His CO_4 count is 54, and western blot test is positive for HIV.

1. The MOST likely diagnosis of this condition is   1.____

    A. cytomegalovirus
    B. mycobacterium aviam intracellulare
    C. histoplasmosis
    D. toxoplasmosis

2. The nurse should do all of the following to protect herself from AIDS infection EXCEPT   2.____

    A. exercise care when handling sharp instruments
    B. use disposable mouthpieces and airways instead of direct mouth to mouth resuscitation
    C. wash gloves before use with another patient
    D. wash hands after removing gloves and between patient contact

3. To improve the nutritional status of the patient, all of the following measures should be   3.____
    adopted EXCEPT

    A. including patient in decision-making process regarding his nutritional care
    B. try to give drugs before meals
    C. encourage patient to maximize nutritional intake during periods when he is feeling better
    D. discourage excessive alcohol intake, which has an immunosuppressive effect

4. Nursing interventions facilitating patient understanding of the goals of therapy and methods to prevent HIV transmission include   4.____

    A. encouraging patient to discuss feelings and concerns about the plan of therapy and changes in work, home, and lifestyle environment
    B. using a nonjudgmental approach during care
    C. warning patient not to share toilet articles or donate blood or organs
    D. all of the above

Questions 5-8.

DIRECTIONS: Questions 5 through 8 are to be answered on the basis of the following information.

A 29-year-old black male has a cough with mucopurulent sputum, hemoptysis, and dyspnea, with a history of low-grade fever, night sweats, and weight loss. His laboratory workup
confirms the diagnosis of pulmonary tuberculosis.

5.   Risk factors for the activation of tuberculosis include all of the following EXCEPT   5.____

   A.   close contact with someone who has infectious tuberculosis
   B.   infection with a sexually transmitted disease
   C.   a tuberculin skin test which has recently converted to a significant reaction
   D.   declining immunity or infection with HIV

6.   Nursing education of this patient would NOT include   6.____

   A.   techniques to control propagation of secretions while coughing
   B.   stressing the need to breathe only filtered, humidified air
   C.   stressing the importance of a nutritious diet
   D.   all of the above

7.   In a preventive treatment plan for tuberculosis, isoniazid prophylaxis should be offered to   7.____
all of the following EXCEPT

   A.   household members and other close associates of potentially infectious tubercu-
lous cases
   B.   persons recently testing negative to tuberculin reaction
   C.   newly infected persons
   D.   persons with past tuberculosis

8.   Complications of isoniazid therapy that a nurse should have in mind when initiating pro-   8.____
phylaxis include all of the following EXCEPT

   A.   persistent paresthesias of the hands and feet
   B.   progressive liver damage
   C.   loss of appetite, fatigue, joint pain, and dark urine
   D.   bone marrow suppression

9.   Nursing guidelines for the prevention of salmonella infections do NOT include   9.____

   A.   washing hands after using the toilet, particularly during illness and carrier states
   B.   raw eggs or egg drinks should not be ingested
   C.   purchase only kosher meats and meat products
   D.   all food from animal sources should be thoroughly cooked

10.   After eating lunch in a roadside restaurant, a patient develops fever, crampy abdominal   10.____
pain, diarrhea, mixed blood and mucus, and profound prostration.
Nursing interventions in the management of this disorder include all of the following
EXCEPT

   A.   assessing patient for dehydration
   B.   offering a caffeinated liquid during acute stage of illness
   C.   assisting in epidemiological study of every patient in whom organism is found
   D.   instructing patient to avoid taking antimotility agents

11. Measures which should be taken in the prevention of this disorder do NOT include   11.____

    A. prophylactic vaccination of all children under 12 years of age
    B. a program of fly control
    C. surveillance of water sanitation
    D. an adequate sewage disposal program

Questions 12-13.

DIRECTIONS: Questions 12 and 13 are to be answered on the basis of the following information.

    After drinking water from a restaurant, a 25-year-old man develops fever, headache, malaise, a non-productive cough, and irregularly spaced small rose-colored spots on his abdomen, chest, and back. His pulse is relatively slow in comparison with his fever.

12. All of the following complications may be expected in this patient EXCEPT   12.____

    A. intestinal hemorrhage and perforation
    B. thrombophelibitis
    C. multiple sclerosis
    D. osteomyelitis

13. Environmental hygiene should be established to prevent enteric fever in endemic areas   13.____
by

    A. avoiding all fresh fruits and vegetables
    B. homogenization of all milk and dairy products
    C. protection and purification of water supplies
    D. all of the above

Questions 14-16.

DIRECTIONS: Questions 14 through 16 are to be answered on the basis of the following information.

    Two days after a 29-year-old male was hit by a car, he develops headache, fever, and becomes hyperirritable and restless, with rigidity of both flexor and extensor muscles. After a thorough laboratory investigation, he is diagnosed with a case of tetanus.

14. Complications that may be expected in this patient include all of the following EXCEPT   14.____

    A. dysrhythmias   B. cerebrovascular accident
    C. cardiac arrest   D. bacterial shock

15. Nursing interventions in preventing respiratory and cardiovascular complications include   15.____
all of the following EXCEPT

    A. monitoring for dysphagia
    B. providing cardiac monitoring
    C. delaying intubation and mechanical ventilation as long as possible if spasms are interfering with respiratory function
    D. maintaining an adequate airway

16. Nursing interventions in the ongoing assessment and support of this patient include

    16.____

    A. placing the patient in a completely dark, soundproof environment to avoid stimulating reflex spasms
    B. watching for excessive urinary output
    C. avoiding sudden stimuli and light as the slightest stimulation may trigger paroxysmal spasms
    D. all of the above

17. Lyme disease is caused by borrelia burgdorferi and is introduced by an ixodid tick. Nursing instructions for people living in or visiting an endemic area would NOT include

    17.____

    A. applying insect repellent
    B. tucking pants into boots or socks
    C. removing tick with forceps, exerting slow, steady upward pull, and avoid squeezing the tick
    D. cut a shallow X across the tick bite with a sterile blade

18. Nursing interventions to make patients aware of sexual practices that will reduce the chances of acquiring a sexually transmitted disease include all of the following EXCEPT

    18.____

    A. avoiding sex with individuals who have had multiple partners
    B. not using water-soluble lubricants
    C. avoiding douching before and after sex
    D. use latex condoms lubricated with nonoxynol-9

19. Diseases that are NOT transmitted via respiratory secretions include

    19.____

    A. tuberculosis   B. AIDS
    C. rubeola   D. rheumatic fever

20. Diseases transmitted via blood and body fluids do NOT include

    20.____

    A. AIDS   B. hepatitis B
    C. hepatitis A   D. all of the above

21. Patients at high risk for social isolation include those infected with

    21.____

    A. tetanus   B. tuberculosis
    C. AIDS   D. all of the above

22. All of the following conditions are prevalent in advanced age EXCEPT

    22.____

    A. osteoporosis   B. scoliosis
    C. cataracts   D. multiple sclerosis

23. Impaired physical mobility related to muscular weakness may be found in patients with

    23.____

    A. Parkinson's disease   B. rheumatoid arthritis
    C. cerebral palsy   D. all of the above

24. Nursing interventions to assist patients in coping with their health problems do NOT include   24.____

    A. referral to support groups
    B. understanding and patience
    C. referral for psychoanalysis
    D. none of the above

25. Patients with, conditions that may be expected to degenerate include those with   25.____

    A. cerebrovascular accidents
    B. multiple sclerosis
    C. spinal cord injuries
    D. all of the above

KEY (CORRECT ANSWERS)

1.	D		11.	A
2.	C		12.	C
3.	B		13.	C
4.	D		14.	B
5.	B		15.	C
6.	B		16.	C
7.	B		17.	D
8.	D		18.	B
9.	C		19.	B
10.	B		20.	C

21. D
22. D
23. A
24. C
25. B

TEST 2

DIRECTIONS: Each question or incomplete statement is followed by several suggested answers or completions. Select the one that BEST answers the question or completes the statement. *PRINT THE LETTER OF THE CORRECT ANSWER IN THE SPACE AT THE RIGHT.*

Questions 1-6.

DIRECTIONS: Questions 1 through 6 are to be answered on the basis of the following information.

A 29-year-old white male has a closed, oblique fracture of the tibia and fibula resulting from a traffic accident.

1. Nursing interventions in the management of this patient involve all of the following EXCEPT

    A. relieving pain and discomfort
    B. promoting complete physical immobilization
    C. preventing the development of disuse syndrome
    D. promoting a positive psychological response to trauma

1.____

2. In the above patient, a closed reduction is done and a cast is applied.
    Nursing interventions to dry a plaster cast properly include all of the following EXCEPT

    A. avoid handling cast when wet, if possible; handle with palms, not fingertips
    B. avoid placing the cast on a hard surface while drying
    C. use a heat lamp or hair dryer to speed drying time
    D. not to completely cover the cast

2.____

3. Nursing care of the patient to maintain good circulation after the cast is applied does NOT include

    A. observing for the five P's (pain, pallor, paralysis, paresthesia, and pulselessness) of neurovascular assessment for muscle ischemia
    B. observing circulatory status in exposed fingers or toes
    C. cutting out pressure areas of the cast on the extremity
    D. all of the above

3.____

4. In this type of fracture, complications associated with immobility include all of the following EXCEPT

    A. loss of muscle strength and endurance
    B. loss of range of motion/joint contracture
    C. pressure sores at bony prominences
    D. muscular hypertrophy

4.____

5. Nursing interventions to aid in preventing development of thromboembolism include

    A. encourage immobility, do not change position frequently, and discourage ambulation
    B. elevate legs to prevent statis, avoiding pressure on blood vessels

5.____

C. avoid elastic stockings or sequential compression devices
D. all of the above

6. In setting the discharge plan, the nurse should advise the patient to   6.____

   A. adjust usual lifestyle and responsibilities to accommodate limitations imposed by fracture
   B. start active exercises and continue with isometric exercises after the cast is removed
   C. carefully limit the amount of weight bearing that will be permitted on the fractured extremity
   D. all of the above

Questions 7-9.

DIRECTIONS: Questions 7 through 9 are to be answered on the basis of the following information.

A 65-year-old female suffers a fracture of the right hip joint after slipping on a wet floor. After thorough evaluation of the case, a total hip replacement is performed.

7. Nursing interventions in promoting the comfort of the patient include all of the following   7.____
EXCEPT

   A. placing a pillow on the outer sides of both the legs to keep affected leg in adduction
   B. with two nurses positioned on each side of the bed, using the draw sheet to lift and reposition the patient in bed
   C. placing the patient in a supine position, placing a pillow under the affected leg from mid-thigh to ankle, keeping the leg in a neutral rotation
   D. handling the affected extremity gently

8. All of the following complications may be suspected in this patient EXCEPT   8.____

   A. pneumonia   B. cardiac arrest
   C. fat emboli   D. infection

9. In discussing the discharge plan with the patient and her family, the nurse should recommend all of the following precautions EXCEPT: 9.____

   A. Do not lift heavy objects
   B. Do not cross or twist legs
   C. Observe carefully for signs of wound infection
   D. Try to sleep on operative side

10. A 20-year-old male has a suspected fracture of the lumbar spine.   10.____
Nursing interventions to avoid complications associated with spinal fracture and immobility do NOT include

   A. measures to prevent risk of thromboembolism complications
   B. monitoring bowel and bladder function
   C. encouraging the patient to ambulate as soon as possible
   D. all of the above

11. Traction is the force applied in a specific direction. Purposes of traction include all of the following EXCEPT   11.____

    A. reduction and immobilization of the fracture
    B. increasing muscle spasms
    C. regaining normal length and alignment of an injured extremity
    D. preventing deformity

12. Nursing interventions in the care of a patient on traction do NOT include   12.____

    A. encouraging deep breathing hourly to facilitate expansion of lungs and movement of respiratory secretions
    B. encouraging active exercise of uninvolved muscles
    C. adding progressively heavier weights to the traction apparatus
    D. that the traction must be continuous to be effective

13. Total hip replacement is indicated in all of the following clinical conditions EXCEPT   13.____

    A. complete dislocation of the hip joint
    B. pathological fractures from metastatic cancer
    C. femoral neck fracture
    D. congenital hip disease

14. A 26-year-old male has an above knee amputation performed after severe traumatic injury.   14.____
Nursing intervention in the education of this patient includes teaching

    A. the patient and his family how to wrap the residual limb with elastic bandage to control edema and to form a firm conical shape for prosthesis fitting
    B. the patient residual limb-conditioning by pushing the residual limb against a soft pillow
    C. methods of care of the residual limb and prosthesis, washing and drying the limb thoroughly at least twice a day, and removing all soap residue to prevent skin irritation or infection
    D. all of the above

15. A patient with multiple myeloma is admitted to the hospital.   15.____
Nursing interventions to prevent pathological fractures include

    A. assisting the patient in movement with gentleness and patience
    B. allowing the joints to bend freely when repositioning the patient
    C. keeping the patient immobile
    D. all of the above

16. A 58-year-old nulliparous white female is admitted for alcohol detoxification. In the assessment of this patient, the nurse notes that she is at high risk for osteoporosis. The nurse should advise the patient all of the following EXCEPT   16.____

    A. dietary supplements to minimize bone mass
    B. participating in dietary education related to vitamin D intake
    C. vigorous exercise
    D. strategies to prevent falls

17. A 38-year-old patient is admitted for rheumatoid arthritis.   17.____
Nursing interventions to aid the patient in adjusting to the chronic nature of this condition include all of the following EXCEPT

    A. advising that continuous immobilization may decrease pain
    B. allowing the patient to express fears and concerns
    C. encouraging continued follow-up to re-evaluate progression of disease and efficacy of drug therapy
    D. teaching the patient to avoid sudden jarring movements of joints

18. Predisposing factors for a herniated lumbar disk include all of the following EXCEPT   18.____

    A. sedentary occupations
    B. frequent physical exercise
    C. long-term driving, e.g., truckdriver
    D. participation in bowling or baseball

19. Nursing interventions to keep a patient with a herniated lumbar disk free of pain include   19.____

    A. bed rest on a firm mattress with bed board; traction as ordered
    B. administering morphine every 6-8 hours
    C. encouraging an exercise program of trunk-twists and deep knee bends
    D. all of the above

20. Indications for surgical intervention in patients with herniated lumbar disks include all of the following EXCEPT   20.____

    A. prevention of further nerve damage and deficits
    B. intermittent back and leg pain
    C. sensory and motor deficits in lower extremities
    D. bowel and bladder dysfunction

Questions 21-23.

DIRECTIONS: Questions 21 through 23 are to be answered on the basis of the following information.

A 25-year-old male sustains an acute head injury after a traffic accident.

21. Nursing interventions for the detection of CSF or blood draining from the nose or ears include all of the following EXCEPT   21.____

    A. observe and record, at least hourly, any leak of blood or clear fluid from the nose or ears
    B. pack nose or ears
    C. immediately report to physician if any drainage is found
    D. drain fluid onto sterile towels or dressings

22. Nursing interventions to keep the patient free from infection or injury include   22.____

    A. seizure precautions
    B. strict aseptic techniques during all invasive procedures
    C. restricting visitors with any respiratory illness
    D. all of the above

23. The patient is undergoing intracranial surgery.   23.____
Nursing interventions to prevent post-operative complications include all of the following EXCEPT

   A. checking ears, nose, and dressings for drainage
   B. suctioning through the nose
   C. supporting head when turning the patient
   D. monitoring breathing, advising the patient that he must not cough

24. A 75-year-old woman is admitted with CVA caused by hemorrhage.   24.____
Nursing interventions in the care of this patient include all of the following EXCEPT

   A. elevating head of the bed 30-45° to improve venous drainage
   B. decreasing environmental stimuli
   C. turning patient gently to the affected side
   D. maintaining complete bedrest until bleeding has been controlled and patient's condition is stable

25. In a patient with Parkinson's disease, nursing interventions to help maintain gastrointestinal integrity include all of the following EXCEPT   25.____

   A. providing adequate fluid intake
   B. restricting carbohydrates
   C. providing a high-fiber diet
   D. administering stool softeners or laxatives as ordered

26. Nursing interventions to maintain positive body image and self-concept would NOT include   26.____

   A. providing clothes that are simple to put on
   B. supervising and assisting in skin care and personal hygiene
   C. installing a mirror that can easily be seen by the patient
   D. all of the above

27. Myasthenia gravis is diagnosed in a 45-year-old white female.   27.____
Nursing interventions to keep the patient free from respiratory impairment include which of the following?

   A. Postural drainage; turning patient frequently
   B. Diaphragmatic breathing exercises to maintain strength with maximum ventilation and minimum energy expenditure
   C. Balancing physical activities with rest
   D. All of the above

28. Nursing care to keep the patient mentioned above well-nourished would NOT include   28.____

   A. providing small, frequent, semisolid or fluid meals that are nutritious and high in potassium
   B. inserting a feeding tube
   C. observing for aspiration; keeping suction equipment available
   D. allowing patient to eat meals without rushing

Questions 29-30.

DIRECTIONS: Questions 29 and 30 are to be answered on the basis of the following informa-
                    tion.
        A 30-year-old white female develops nystagmus, intentional tremors, and spastic weak-
ness of limbs. She also has a history of sudden falls while standing, dropping things out of
her hands, and urinary incontinence. After a thorough diagnostic work-up, she is diagnosed
with multiple sclerosis.

29.   Nursing interventions in this case do NOT include   29._____

        A.   encouraging optimal activity level
        B.   promoting adequate rest periods to prevent exhaustion
        C.   providing self-help devices for eating, ambulation, and reading
        D.   restraining patient while in bed

30.   Nursing interventions to make the patient clearly under stand and express her fears do   30._____
        NOT include

        A.   talking to the patient and family together and separately
        B.   encouraging patient to begin psychotherapy treatment
        C.   allowing expression of depression and hopelessness
        D.   clarifying misconceptions and lack of information about present status and progno-
              sis

_____

KEY (CORRECT ANSWERS)

1.	B	11.	B
2.	C	12.	C
3.	C	13.	A
4.	D	14.	D
5.	B	15.	A
6.	D	16.	A
7.	A	17.	A
8.	B	18.	B
9.	D	19.	A
10.	C	20.	B
21.	B	26.	C
22.	D	27.	D
23.	B	28.	B
24.	C	29.	D
25.	B	30.	B

_____

EXAMINATION SECTION
TEST 1

DIRECTIONS: Each question or incomplete statement is followed by several suggested answers or completions. Select the one that BEST answers the question or completes the statement. *PRINT THE LETTER OF THE CORRECT ANSWER IN THE SPACE AT THE RIGHT.*

1. The purpose of treating Parkinson's disease with Levodopa is to   1.____

    A. increase the production of acetylcholine
    B. replace dopamine in the brain cells
    C. improve the myelination of the neurons of the basal ganglia
    D. regenerate the neurons of the basal ganglia

2. Which of the following is NOT a possible major side effect of tetracyclines?   2.____

    A. Impaired kidney function
    B. Bone defects (in small children)
    C. Phototoxicity
    D. Neurotoxicity

3. Which of the following drugs may be prescribed for the prevention and treatment of gout?   3.____

    A. Acetominophen   B. Hydrocortisone
    C. Colchicine   D. Ibuprofen

4. A client with tetanus should be observed closely for   4.____

    A. pallor and perspiration
    B. respiratory spasms
    C. muscled rigidity
    D. involuntary muscle spasms

5. Vomiting should NOT be induced for poisonings involving   5.____

    A. acetaminophen   B. petroleum distillates
    C. plant parts   D. salicylate

6. After a spinal cord injury, a client should be encourated to drink fluids in order to   6.____

    A. prevent meningal infections
    B. avoid gangrene
    C. prevent urinary tract infections
    D. balance fluids and electrolytes

7. A nurse should use a tilt table in treating an arthritic client in order to   7.____

    A. prevent pressure ulcers
    B. prevent calcium loss
    C. promote spinal hyperextension
    D. prevent muscular atrophy

8. For an unimmunized 14-month-old, initial immunizations would include each of the following EXCEPT   8.____

    A. oral poliovirus vaccine   B. DTP
    C. Td   D. tuberculin test

9. Which lobe of the cerebral cortex is responsible for registering general sensations of heat, cold, pain, and touch?   9.____

    A. Occipital   B. Parietal   C. Temporal   D. Frontal

10. A client is admitted to the emergency room with a sucking stab wound on the right side of the thorax. Into what position should the nurse place the client?   10.____

    A. On the back, with the head elevated
    B. In a high-Fowler's position with the right side supported
    C. On the left side, flat, with a pillow supporting the left arm
    D. On the right side, with the head elevated

11. The FIRST symptom of open-angle glaucoma is   11.____

    A. persistent headaches
    B. continually blurred vision
    C. uncontrollable twitching of the eye
    D. impaired peripheral vision

12. Respiratory isolation would be recommended for a client with   12.____

    A. cholera   B. diphtheria
    C. laryngeal tuberculosis   D. meningitis

13. The diet for a client being treated for ulcerative colitis may include each of the following EXCEPT   13.____

    A. raw bran   B. milk
    C. hot cereal   D. sliced apple

14. Which of the following is a common early symptom of myasthenia gravis?   14.____

    A. Blurred vision   B. Double vision
    C. Migraine headaches   D. Tearing

15. A client taking ampicillin at home should notify the physician   15.____

    A. if diarrhea develops
    B. when symptoms disappear entirely
    C. when a negative culture is obtained
    D. if drowsiness occurs

16. If a client experiences a generalized motor seizure, the nurse's primary responsibility is to   16.____

    A. insert a plastic airway between the teeth
    B. restrain the client's movements for safety
    C. clear the immediate environment for safety
    D. administer the prescribed anticonvulsant

17. For what purpose are clients encouraged to perform deep breathing exercises following   17._____
surgery?

    A. Increasing cardiac output
    B. Expanding residual volume
    C. Increasing blood volume
    D. Counteracting respiratory acidosis

18. Which of the following would be experienced by a client with multiple sclerosis?   18._____

    A. Tremors
    C. Mental confusion
    B. Double vision
    D. Respiratory congestion

19. To reduce the risk of toxoplasmosis, pregnant women should be taught to avoid   19._____

    A. cleaning the cat box
    B. unprotected sex
    C. stagnant pools of water
    D. eating marine animals

20. For a client who has just undergone an above-the-knee amputation, the nurse should   20._____
work to avoid a hip contracture by

    A. making sure the client lies in the prone position several times a day
    B. making sure the client sits in a chair frequently throughout the day
    C. propping the stump with pillows
    D. elevating the head of the client's bed

21. Following the repair of an inguinal hernia, the nurse can BEST help the recovering client   21._____
by

    A. applying an abdominal binder
    B. encouraging frequent coughing
    C. placing a rolled towel under the scrotum
    D. encouraging a high-carbohydrate diet

22. Which of the following would MOST likely be discovered during a nursing assessment of   22._____
a client with Meniere's disease?

    A. Hypotension
    B. Diplopia
    C. Hearing loss
    D. Jerky lateral eye movement

23. Due to concern for the development of blackwater fever, a client with malaria should be   23._____
closely observed for

    A. dark red urine
    C. vomiting
    B. low-grade fever
    D. nausea

24. Which of the following substances is released by axons supplying skeletal muscles?   24._____

    A. Potassium
    C. ATP
    B. Acetylcholine
    D. Epinephrine

25. Which of the following is NOT considered to be an antimicrobial secretion of the human   25.____
    body?

    A. Tears   B. Gastric juice
    C. Mucus   D. Vaginal secretions

KEY (CORRECT ANSWERS)

1.	B		11.	D
2.	D		12.	D
3.	B		13.	B
4.	B		14.	B
5.	B		15.	A
6.	C		16.	C
7.	B		17.	D
8.	C		18.	B
9.	C		19.	A
10.	D		20.	A

21.	C
22.	D
23.	A
24.	B
25.	C

TEST 2

DIRECTIONS: Each question or incomplete statement is followed by several suggested answers or completions. Select the one that BEST answers the question or completes the statement. *PRINT THE LETTER OF THE CORRECT ANSWER IN THE SPACE AT THE RIGHT.*

1.   Which of the following is the MOST likely cause of osteoporosis?   1._____

   A.   Iron deficiency
   B.   Prolonged inactivity
   C.   Prolonged period of low WBC
   D.   Estrogen therapy

2.   Which of the following is an early sign of lead poisoning in children?   2._____

   A.   Mental confusion   B.   Anemia
   C.   Tremors   D.   Yellow sclerae

3.   If a client's mouth appears pulled to the right, it is an indication of injury to the _____   3._____
     nerve.

   A.   left vestibular   B.   left trigeminal
   C.   right abducent   D.   right facial

4.   Which of the following medications would NOT be used to treat gangrene?   4._____

   A.   Tetracycline   B.   Chloramphenicol
   C.   Streptomycin sulfate   D.   Penicillin G

5.   Which of the following would be experienced by a client with tic dolourex, or trigeminal   5._____
     neuralgia?

   A.   Yellow sclerae
   B.   Uncontrollable twitching of eyelid
   C.   Unilateral muscle paralysis
   D.   Extreme head and facial pain

6.   Following a laminectomy, which of the following is the primary postoperative complication   6._____
     that should be observed for?

   A.   Cerebral edema
   B.   Compression of spinal cord
   C.   Bladder spasms
   D.   Increased intracranial pressure

7.   Each of the following results from a streptococci infection that enters via the upper respi-   7._____
     ratory tract EXCEPT

   A.   mononucleosis   B.   puerperal sepsis
   C.   rheumatic fever   D.   shigellosis

8.   After being admitted to the emergency room for injuries sustained in a serious automo-   8._____
     bile accident, a client undergoes a splenectomy. In the immediate postoperative period,
     the nurse should watch for

A. intestinal bleeding or obstruction
B. peritonitis
C. hemorrhage or distended abdomen
D. infection or shock

9. What type of stool should be expected from a client that has a colostomy on the left side   9.____
   of the abdomen?

   A. Coated with stringy mucus
   B. Bloody
   C. Moist and formed
   D. Liquid

10. In bites involving the lower extremities, the incubation period for rabies is about   10.____

    A. 10 days   B. 40 days   C. 2 months   D. 4 months

11. Clients with spinal cord injuries sometimes experience sympathetic hyperreflexia. Each   11.____
    of the following is a sign or symptom of this condition EXCEPT

    A. pulsating headache   B. goose bumps
    C. pallor   D. diaphoresis

12. Which of the following positions would be appropriate for a client suffering from cerebral   12.____
    thrombosis?

    A. Semi-Fowler's   B. Sims'
    C. Trendlenburg   D. Prone

13. A diagnosis of *thrush* actually refers to a(n)   13.____

    A. acid-fast bacterial infection
    B. protozoan parasite
    C. virus
    D. yeast infection

14. Osteoarthritis is MOST likely to involve the joints of the   14.____

    A. metacarpals and fingers   B. knees and hips
    C. shoulders and elbows   D. metatarsals and ankles

15. Which of the following laboratory tests would be helpful in confirming a diagnosis of sys-   15.____
    temic lupus erythematosus?

    A. WBC   B. Blood pH
    C. Blood gases   D. BUN

16. Which of the following is NOT a therapeutic intervention involved in the treatment of teta-   16.____
    nus?

    A. Penicillin G
    B. Diazepam to limit spasms
    C. Cleansing of would with aqueous benzalkonium chloride
    D. Wound debridement to allow exposure to air

17. A client experiencing left hemiplagia following a cerebral vascular accident would suffer   17.____
    paralysis of each of the following EXCEPT the

    A. left arm   B. left eyelid
    C. left leg   D. right side of the face

18. Which of the following, observed in a client, would indicate malaria?   18.____

    A. Erythrocytosis
    B. Leukocytosis
    C. Splenomegaly
    D. Increased sedimentation rate

19. Which of the following side effects may be a consequence of treating cerebral edema   19.____
    with dexamethasone?

    A. Involuntary muscle contracture
    B. Hypotension
    C. Increased intracranial pressure
    D. Hyperglycemia

20. *Full-thickness* burns are so classified because they have extended to involve damage to   20.____
    the

    A. epidermis   B. upper dermis
    C. subcutaneous layer   D. muscular tissue

21. The MAJOR problem encountered by newly paraplegic clients is   21.____

    A. atrophy
    B. control of the bladder
    C. ambulation
    D. formation of urinary calculi

22. When the spinal cord is crushed above the level of the phrenic nerve origin, _____ will   22.____
    result.

    A. respiratory paralysis
    B. vagus nerve dysfunction
    C. cardiac arrhythmia
    D. retention of sensation in lower extremities

23. An adolescent epileptic client who has been taking Dilantin develops status epilepticus.   23.____
    The MOST likely reason for this is that the

    A. prescribed dosage of Dilantin was insufficient for the client's activity level
    B. client failed to take the prescribed dosage consistently
    C. client has built up a tolerance for the prescribed dosage
    D. seizures are becoming more intense in response to the prescribed dosage

24. The test that is performed immediately to confirm a diagnosis of meningitis is   24._____

    A. blood culture   B. lumbar puncture
    C. meningomyelogram   D. alkaline phosphatase

25. Which of the following is the relay center for sensory impulses?   25._____

    A. Thalamus   B. Cerebellum
    C. Medulla oblongata   D. Pons

KEY (CORRECT ANSWERS)

1. B		11. C
2. B		12. B
3. D		13. D
4. C		14. B
5. D		15. D
6. B		16. C
7. D		17. B
8. C		18. C
9. C		19. D
10. D		20. C

21. B
22. A
23. B
24. B
25. A

TEST 3

DIRECTIONS: Each question or incomplete statement is followed by several suggested answers or completions. Select the one that BEST answers the question or completes the statement. *PRINT THE LETTER OF THE CORRECT ANSWER IN THE SPACE AT THE RIGHT.*

1. What type of antibiotics operate by blocking tRNA attachment to cell ribosomes?   1.____

   A. Tetracyclines   B. Erythromycins
   C. Cephalosporins   D. Penicillins

2. The primary goal of the medical treatment of chronic glaucoma is   2.____

   A. preventing secondary infections
   B. pupil dilation
   C. increasing ocular range of motion
   D. the control of intraocular pressure

3. A client with a peptic ulcer would be permitted to eat or drink each of the following EXCEPT   3.____

   A. milk   B. oatmeal
   C. applesauce   D. orange juice

4. After a fracture of the hip, what is/are the MOST frequently developed contracture(s)?   4.____

   A. Flexion and adduction of the hip
   B. Hyperextension of the knee
   C. External rotation
   D. Internal rotation

5. Which of the following clinical findings would NOT support a diagnosis of Crohn's disease?   5.____

   A. Occult blood in stool
   B. Anemia
   C. Elevated WBC
   D. Severe pain in right lower quadrant

6. Which of the following produce antibodies?   6.____

   A. Erythrocytes   B. Plasma cells
   C. Eosiniphils   D. Lymphocytes

7. Which of the following is NOT a common cause of gastritis?   7.____

   A. Chronic uremia
   B. Allergic reactions
   C. Zollinger-Ellison syndrome
   D. Bacterial or viral infection

8. When administering chloramphenicol to an infected client, a nurse should   8.____

   A. observe for anticoagulant effect
   B. observe for neuromuscular blockage

C. assess blood work before and during therapy
D. be watchful for false positive urine tests

9. A client with rheumatoid arthritis should be taught to   9._____

    A. maintain the limbs in a position of extension
    B. place pillows beneath the knees
    C. remain in a semi-Fowler's position as long as possible
    D. assume positions that are most comfortable

10. A client, who was earlier admitted with multiple serious injuries sustained in an accident,   10._____
    is diagnosed with a stress ulcer. The nurse should watch for, and immediately report,

    A. nausea and headache
    B. diaphoresis and cold extremities
    C. diarrhea and distention
    D. warm, flushed skin and complaints of thirst

11. Because of the behavior of damaged cells, clients with serious burns should have levels   11._____
    of _____ checked frequently.

    A. vitamin A   B. sodium
    C. potassium   D. calcium

12. Injury or infection of the _____ nerve is MOST likely to be the cause of nerve deafness.   12._____

    A. facial   B. trigeminal
    C. cochlear   D. vestibular

13. Each of the following is a symptom of severe cinchonism EXCEPT   13._____

    A. deafness   B. blood in the urine
    C. severe nausea   D. vertigo

14. The irreversible effects of untreated lead poisoning are imposed mainly upon the _____   14._____
    system.

    A. lymphatic   B. digestive
    C. urinary   D. central nervous

15. Which of the following signs would indicate developing thrombophlebitis following pelvic   15._____
    surgery?

    A. Edematous ankles
    B. A painful, tender area on the leg
    C. A reddened area at ankle and knee joints
    D. Pruritis on the thigh

16. Which of the following would increase a client's risk of osteoporosis?   16._____

    A. A history of hyperparathyroidism
    B. Long-term steroid therapy
    C. Excessive estrogen consumption
    D. Frequent strenuous physical activity

17. What is the term for an internal antimicrobial protein agent that destroys certain gram-negative bacteria and viruses?

    A. Properdin   B. Lysozyme
    C. Amantadine   D. Interferon

17.____

18. Nerve fibers that are destroyed in the brain or spinal cord do not regenerate because they do not have

    A. nuclei   B. a sodium pump
    C. a neurilemma   D. a myelin sheath

18.____

19. Which crutch gait should be taught to a client fitted with a prosthesis after a single leg amputation?

    A. Three-point   B. Four-point
    C. Swing-through   D. Tripod

19.____

20. After surgery of the biliary tract, clients are at risk for developing respiratory infections because

    A. bile in the blood causes lowered resistance
    B. pathogens are transferred from bile to the blood
    C. the incision is adjacent to the diaphragm
    D. the anesthesia involved in lengthy surgery weakens immunity

20.____

21. When assessing a client suspected for increased intra-cranial pressure, the nurse may expect to discover any of the following EXCEPT

    A. rapid pulse rate   B. psychotic behavior
    C. nausea or vomiting   D. impaired pupil reactivity

21.____

22. When an organism enters a wound and produces a toxin which causes crepitus, what disease has been produced?

    A. Salmonella   B. Botulism
    C. Gas gangrene   D. Tetanus

22.____

23. Which of the following laboratory tests should a nurse refer to in order to aid in the diagnosis of arthritis?

    A. Creatinine level   B. Bence Jones protein
    C. Antinuclear antibody   D. Sodium level

23.____

24. Which of the following is a characteristic manifestation of rabies?

    A. Confusion or memory loss
    B. Pharyngeal spasm
    C. Echolalia
    D. Diarrhea

24.____

25. Which of the following assessment findings would NOT support a diagnosis of hiatal hernia?

    A. Nocturnal dyspnea   B. Regurgitation
    C. Respiratory pain   D. Heartburn after eating

25.____

KEY (CORRECT ANSWERS)

1.	A		11.	C
2.	D		12.	C
3.	D		13.	B
4.	A		14.	D
5.	A		15.	B
6.	B		16.	B
7.	C		17.	A
8.	C		18.	C
9.	A		19.	B
10.	D		20.	C

21.	A
22.	C
23.	C
24.	B
25.	C

TEST 4

DIRECTIONS: Each question or incomplete statement is followed by several suggested answers or completions. Select the one that BEST answers the question or completes the statement. *PRINT THE LETTER OF THE CORRECT ANSWER IN THE SPACE AT THE RIGHT.*

1. Which of the following is considered to be the MOST common complication of peptic ulcer?

    A. Varices of the esophagus
    B. Perforation
    C. Hemorrhage
    D. Pyloric stenosis

    1.____

2. A client is admitted to the emergency room following a serious automobile accident in which she suffered head injuries. Soon after admission, her temperature is measured at 102.6°F.
   This suggests an injury to the

    A. pons Varolii   B. optic chiasm
    C. temporal lobe   D. hypothalamus

    2.____

3. Which of the following side effects may be experienced by a client taking sulfonamides for treatment of a urinary tract infection?

    A. Diarrhea   B. Fatigue
    C. Photosensitivity   D. Nephrotoxicity

    3.____

4. A client suffering from myasthenia gravis would receive a dosage of neostigmine in order to

    A. accelerate neural transmission
    B. block the action of cholinesterase
    C. stimulate the cerebral cortex
    D. boost immunity

    4.____

5. When tetracycline is given orally, it should be given

    A. an hour before milk or dairy products are ingested
    B. with a meal or snack
    C. with an antacid
    D. with orange juice or other citrus juice

    5.____

6. 48 hours after a cerebral vascular accident, the client should begin

    A. exercises designed to actively return muscle function
    B. isometric exercises
    C. active exercises of all extremities
    D. passive range-of-motion exercises

    6.____

7. Following surgery, a client's feedings are administered by nasogastric tube. Shortly after the feedings begin, the client develops diarrhea.
   Which of the following is a possible solution?

    7.____

A. Decreasing the carbohydrate content of the formula
B. Decreasing the protein content of the formula
C. Diluting the formula with water
D. Switching to IV feedings

8. Which of the following is a common side effect associated with Dilantin? 8.____

    A. Facial tics   B. Impaired pupil response
    C. Tinnitus   D. Hypertrophy of the gums

9. Contact isolation would be imposed on a client with each of the following infections 9.____
   EXCEPT

    A. impetigo
    B. chickenpox
    C. herpes simplex
    D. acute respiratory infections in children

10. A client with an ileostomy would normally present a stool that is 10.____

    A. solid and clay-colored   B. flecked with blood
    C. liquid   D. pencil-shaped

11. When caring for a child with acute laryngitis, the nurse's main concern should be 11.____

    A. reduction of fever
    B. constant delivery of 40% humidified oxygen
    C. increased fluid intake
    D. constant respiratory monitoring

12. Which of the following medications is used to treat tic dolourex, or trigeminal neuralgia? 12.____

    A. Morphine sulfate   B. Carbamazepine
    C. Halol   D. Allopurinol

13. A client who suffered a spinal cord injury three weeks earlier suffers from coffee-ground 13.____
    emesis and restlessness. The nurse should

    A. check hemoglobin levels in laboratory reports
    B. insert a nasogastric tube
    C. change the client to a liquid diet
    D. check for occult blood in the stool

14. Following a splenectomy, a client should be observed carefully for the depletion of 14.____

    A. vitamin A   B. potassium
    C. calcium   D. sodium

15. A nurse could expect each of the following clinical findings from a client with Lyme dis- 15.____
    ease EXCEPT

    A. swollen joints   B. enlarged spleen
    C. lack of coordination   D. paralysis

16. By what route do meningitis-producing bacteria enter the central nervous system?   16.____

 A. Sinuses   B. Pores
 C. Gastrointestinal tract   D. Urinary tract

17. Which of the following results from a Group A beta-hemolytic streptococcal infection?   17.____

 A. Mononucleosis   B. Rheumatic fever
 C. Rheumatoid arthritis   D. Hepatitis A

18. Which of the following drugs is MOST commonly used to treat rheumatoid arthritis?   18.____

 A. Gold salts   B. Hydrocortisone
 C. Aspirin   D. Ibuprofen

19. Worsening colitis is often treated by placing the patient on a bland, residue-free diet and   19.____
 by administering vitamins parenterally. The purpose of this treatment is to

 A. increase intestinal absorption
 B. reduce gastric acidity
 C. minimize colonic irritation
 D. boost electrolytes

20. Stump shrinkage following an amputation is caused by muscular atrophy and   20.____

 A. subcutaneous fat reduction
 B. postoperative edema
 C. loss of bone tissue
 D. skin turgor

21. During a client's early post-burn phase, the nurse's PRIMARY objective should be to   21.____

 A. restore fluid volume   B. initiate tissue repair
 C. relieve pain   D. prevent infection

22. Which of the following would NOT typically be part of a nursing care plan for a client with   22.____
 systemic lupus erythematosus?

 A. Dosages of vitamin C
 B. Renal dialysis
 C. Administration of corticosteroids
 D. Avoiding exposure to sunlight

23. Which of the following is a serious complication of acute malaria?   23.____

 A. Fluid and electrolyte imbalance
 B. Lung congestion
 C. Seizure of peristalsis
 D. Anemia

24. Gold salts used to treat rhematoid arthritis involve the serious side effect of   24.____

 A. emboli
 B. gastric pain
 C. decreased cardiac output
 D. kidney damage

25. Which of the following is NOT a gram-negative, rod-shaped bacteria?   25.____

    A. Shigella   B. Neisseria
    C. Escherichia   D. Salmonella

KEY (CORRECT ANSWERS)

1.	C	11.	D
2.	D	12.	B
3.	C	13.	A
4.	B	14.	B
5.	A	15.	B
6.	D	16.	A
7.	A	17.	B
8.	D	18.	C
9.	B	19.	C
10.	C	20.	A

21.	A
22.	B
23.	A
24.	D
25.	B

Made in the USA
Middletown, DE
30 August 2024

60053555R00073